BRITISH MUSEUM PATTERN BOOKS

African Designs

African Designs

REBECCA JEWELL

Published by British Museum Press

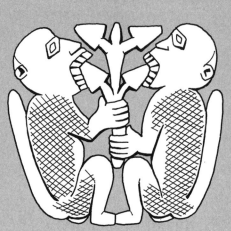

© 1994 Rebecca Jewell

Second impression 1995

Published by British Museum
Press
A division of The British
Museum Company Ltd
46 Bloomsbury Street
London WC1B 3QQ

British Library Cataloguing in
Publication Data.
A catalogue record for this book
is available from the British
Library

ISBN 0–7141–8074–2

Designed by Roger Davies

Typeset by Create Publishing
Services Ltd.
Printed in Great Britain by
The Bath Press, Avon

Acknowledgements

My greatest thanks are due to
Eva Wilson, author of the other
books in this series, who gave
me the initial idea and the
encouragement to study
African patterns. I am very
grateful to Dr John Mack,
Director of the Museum of
Mankind, for allowing me
access to the vast collections of
African material, and for
his advice and comments on the
book. I thank the many
members of staff at the
Museum who helped me, in
particular Julie Hudson, and
also Chris Spring, Dr Nigel
Barley and Jim Hammill.
Special thanks also go to John
Picton at the School of Oriental
and African Studies, for advice
at the outset. Finally, my thanks
are also due to my family for
their support and help.

Contents

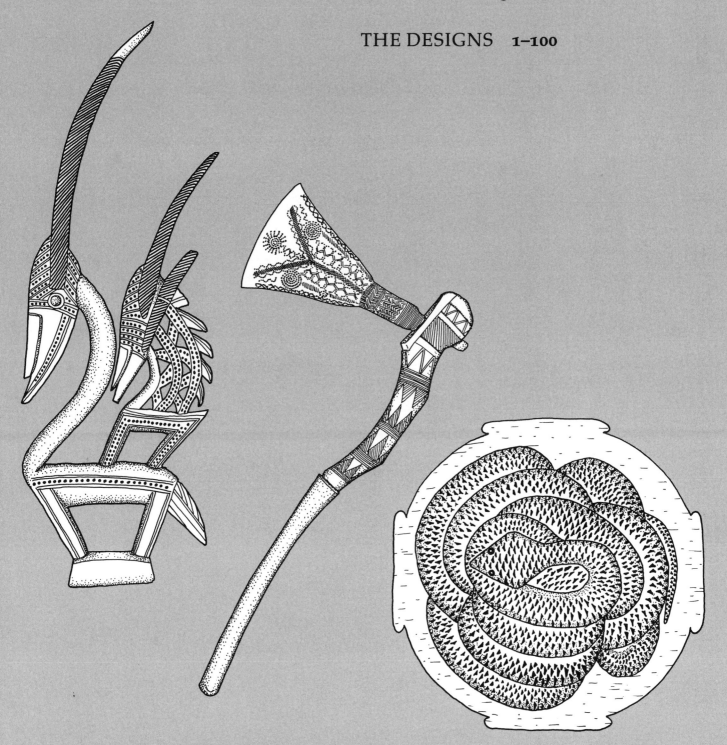

Introduction

This book is one in a series of pattern books published by British Museum Press. It is produced at a time when there is a growing interest in the study of African art. There are more exhibitions being put on in museums and art galleries than ever before – of African textiles, of the work of contemporary African sculptors and artists and of African traditional crafts collected over the last few hundred years. Many contemporary textiles produced by fashion designers in the West take designs and motifs from traditional African cloths. The colourful telephone wire basket and beadwork jewellery from South Africa are sold in craft shops throughout Europe and America, and long strings of African bead necklaces are popular.

This book is a study of African patterns primarily from an artist's point of view. Most of the objects have come from the collections of the Museum of Mankind, the Ethnography Department of the British Museum. Others have come from private collections, books and catalogues. I have tried to reproduce a representative range of images, shapes and textures, found on, or incorporated within, wood, metal, pottery, gourds, textiles, basketware and ivory. The aim has been to provide a pictorial record of many of the decorated objects and textiles in the collections of the Museum of Mankind and to produce a source book for practising artists, potters, textile designers, teachers, art historians, social historians and others interested in African visual culture.

Many of the patterns will be familiar to the expert on African art, as they have been reproduced in photographs in other publications. However, I have also tried to include less familiar patterns and designs which have never been exhibited or published before, for example the finely woven mats from the Congo which are part of the Wellcome collection at the Museum of Mankind (see **83**). Objects have been chosen for their aesthetic value and for their ability to work well when reproduced on paper in black ink. There is a large amount of excellent literature on African textiles and since the majority of textiles with patterns are multicoloured and reproduce better in photographs than in drawings, I have included only a few examples. I have illustrated the kinds of patterns produced by the four main textile techniques – weaving, dying, embroidery, and appliqué. A fifth technique, ikat (dying part of the yarn before it is woven) is only practised in a very few regions of Africa.

I have tried to reproduce patterns as close to the original as possible. However, there is inevitably some degree of interpretation. Many of the carved images on wood, such as the border pattern on the Yoruba door panels (**30–33**) and the decoration on the sides of the wooden boxes from Ghana (**40–43**) are cut in such a way that the light falling on the different angles of the wood gives an added dimension to the overall effect of the design. Where some of these aspects may be lost in an ink drawing, I hope that the reader still gets some feel for the original piece. I have generally drawn circular objects, such as the brass dishes, baskets, calabash, stools with round seats and hats from Senegal or The Gambia, from an aerial view. For flat objects, such as the top of the hats (**52**), or the leather cushions (**23**) this does not pose a problem with the pattern, but for bowl-shapes, such as the gourds (**22** and **44**) and the Sudanese bowls (**17**), this does mean that the edges are distorted and the patterns around the rim would in fact be more elongated if viewed from the side.

There is no single unifying feature which characterises African patterns but rather they are significant for their diversity. Humans and animals are frequently represented, both figuratively and stylistically, and the tendency to distort natural forms for the purpose of emphasising certain characteristics leads to the repeated use of geometric forms. Triangles, diamonds, squares and chevrons (zigzags) appear again and again, from textiles to wood to pottery. Often geometric patterns are given names suggestive of a perceived visual relationship between the pattern and an animal. Some of the earliest rock art of southern Africa, dating to around 10,000 BC, can be divided into categories of figurative representations – animals and people – and geometric designs.

In an attempt to give context to this diversity, I have grouped the drawings mainly according to their geographical region of origin.

North and Northeast Africa

From the first century AD religion had a significant impact on the development of the arts in northern Africa. Christianity was officially recognised there in AD 313, and Coptic art developed in Egypt and spread to Nubia and Ethiopia. But Islam was to overrun Christianity except in the Ethiopian Highlands, where it still survives today.

The Islamic faith entered Egypt from Arabia in 639 AD. It spread to the Maghreb (Morocco, Algeria and Tunisia) and followed the trade routes down the east coast, reaching Madagascar in the ninth century and west Africa by the eleventh century. Where Islam developed, so architecture became a predominant art form, because of the need for communal Friday prayer in a mosque. Distinctive interlacing Islamic designs are found on tiles and pottery in Morocco (6–8) and jewellery from Algeria and Morocco incorporates many of the Islamic symbols such as the hand or 'Khamsa' (meaning 'five' in Arabic) (5). The influence of Islam in Ethiopia can be seen in the beautiful illuminated manuscripts which survive today, most from the seventeenth and eighteenth centuries, but some possibly dating from as early as the fifteenth century. These are characterised by their bold colour – bright reds, blues, yellows and greens – and their vivid figurative scenes. Colourful borders and headbands and plaited bands between chapters decorate the pages (14–15).

Metalwork was an ancient craft in Ethiopia. The arrival of Christianity gave an impetus to the art and the distinctive Ethiopian cross was developed. There were different centres of production, which excelled at different periods, and the styles varied according to region and the type of metal used. The fifteenth-century cross on 13 comes from Gojjam and is made from silver.

West Africa

The Portuguese were among the first far-distant outsiders to explore the west coast of Africa, seeking to control the trade in gold, ivory and pepper. They landed in Sierra Leone in 1460 and in the kingdom of Benin in 1485. They imported, among other things, red coral beads from the Mediterranean, which were worn only by the Benin king. The picture on 63 shows the king wearing a thick coral necklace. Gold was traded in exchange for brass bracelets and copper.

The Portuguese significantly influenced the art of the region. They commissioned carved ivory oliphants, salt-cellars, spoons, forks and dagger handles from the Sapi and Benin craftsmen. The bronze (or rather brass) Benin plaques in the British Museum were made after the Portuguese arrived, and images of the Portuguese in sixteenth-century costume, including European military dress, figure in the plaques regularly (**67**). They are distinguishable by their long hair, pointed noses and beards and are also represented in a more stylised form as on **61**. The plaques reveal the development of artistic techniques, the earliest showing static figures, in full frontal view, the later ones depicting people in profile shooting guns, showing how the craftsmen were tackling new problems in form.

The arts of West Africa today have been significantly influenced from the north. In particular Islam has had an impact on the iconography of designs and patterns. It is traditionally thought that Islam prohibits figurative representations in art, but this has not necessarily led to the demise of representational forms in West Africa. Anthropologists have found that indigenous cults and the Muslim religion can coexist, sometimes merging, and Islam has been able to spread over so much of Africa partly because of this ability to tolerate rather than to overrun indigenous cultures.

Central Africa

From the thirteenth to the fourteenth centuries the vast coastal kingdom of Kongo (now northern Angola, western Zaire and the Southern Republic of Congo) flourished, producing many beautifully decorated textiles, mats, baskets and carved wooden figures, distinctive for their elaborate geometric patterns. Velvet pile cloths (see **80**) were highly sought after once 'discovered' by the Portuguese who arrived there in the late fifteenth century, and along with the Sapi carved ivories, were amongst the first African artefacts to be brought to Europe at the beginning of the sixteenth century.

As in Sierra Leone and Benin, craftsmen were commissioned to carve ivories. Central Africa was most exposed to European influence and the work of Portuguese Catholic missionaries, and many of the ivories are carved with crucifixes, the Madonna, saints and Europeans in sixteenth-century European dress. Christian symbols are intermingled with African ones, and incorporated into traditional rituals and customs.

By the end of the sixteenth century, however, these central African kingdoms were in decline, and during the seventeenth century smaller states arose further east on the fringes of the Congo rain forest. One of these was the Kuba kingdom, centred on the Kasai and Sankuru Rivers of present-day Zaire. Art here centred around the court, where people resisted European influences, not only because the items they valued most highly – their textiles, swords and carvings – could not be surpassed by European imports, but also because of their relative isolation. The Hungarian ethnographer Emil Torday brought back a large number of items from this region for the British Museum between 1904 and 1910, and these were readily accepted by the British public because of the 'accessible' form of the sculptures and the appealing decorative patterns (**81**).

East Africa and Southern Africa

Art forms produced throughout Africa are broadly related to the geography and economy of the area and the way of life of the people. Pastoralists, like the Maasai in Kenya, who herd their animals across large distances, tend not to have developed traditions of sculpture, metal-casting and house decoration. Instead, their art is portable – decorated gourds, painted shields, body painting and jewellery.

South-eastern Africa is more fertile and is divided into chiefdoms, with mixed economies of herding and farming. In Zimbabwe, Transvaal and parts of the Orange Free State, art extends to stone architecture. This architecture reached its summit in the building of the city of Great Zimbabwe. At its most powerful in the mid-fourteenth century the city housed 10,000 people supported by rich economies of cattle rearing, iron smelting, copper work and gold mining. But for reasons not fully understood, the power of the city began to decline and by 1500 trade had ceased and the population had dispersed. The huge stone walls at Great Zimbabwe probably fortified the centre of political power and control. Many of the walls were patterned in different styles according to the period when they were built. Sculptured soapstone bird figures were found on pillars and this bird is now the emblem of Zimbabwe. The craft of stone carving has recently re-emerged in Zimbabwe and there are now many sculptors learning the technique.

The earliest inhabitants of south-eastern Africa, the hunter-gatherers, lived for many years alongside the settled chiefdoms, sometimes working for them by collecting firewood and performing rain-making ceremonies. Rock art, whether painting or engraving, is generally associated with hunter-gatherer economies in the dry regions, although the Bantu-speaking farmers and the pastoralists in southern Africa may have done some of the painting which survives today. As the Dutch migrated into southern Africa from 1652 onwards, they took land from the pastoralists and clashed with the farmers, killing many of them on their way. From the 1830s, the region was thrown into turmoil with the Zulu expansion and the Boer migration into the area. Against this background, beadwork, basket work and mural painting on houses continued to evolve throughout the nineteenth century.

Madagascar was settled before AD 1000 by immigrants originally from Southeast Asia and the nearby African shores. A wealth of different influences, among them Indian, Arabian and Indonesian, resulted in the development of distinctive artistic styles and architecture. These influences also affected the making and design of textiles, which were woven in silk, wool, raffia, cotton, bark and even pineapple and banana fibres.

A History of African Art

African art has been classified in the past in two ways – by the tribe from which it originated and by its use or function. However, art historians and anthropologists no longer use the term 'tribe' because of the difficulty in defining it. The fluid boundaries of political and linguistic groups were fossilised by colonialism and its attempt to force people into artificial groups. A 'tribe' implies a distinct group of people, who speak the same language, have the same social and political structure and the same social values, and yet societies in Africa are often divided, as elsewhere, by class, religion, politics, language and literacy. These divisions lead to the development of different art forms, as to some extent with the Kuba kingdom in Zaire where there was an exclusive royal art, and in Benin, where provincial imitations of court art developed. The classification of art by tribe tends to obscure these differences. Furthermore, in some cases an object may have been traded or commissioned from another artist living many miles away, or from itinerant artists. The Asante in Ghana have for many centuries commissioned the beautifully woven *khasa* (blankets) and *kerka* (wall hangings) from the Fulani weavers in the north (near the Niger river in Mali), and possession of these items is held in very high esteem.

The embroidered gowns from northern Nigeria (**24**) provide a good example of an item being constructed by craftsmen from a number of different ethnic groups – the cloth is woven by one, and the decorated pocket at the front is embroidered by another. The designs for embroidery may be drawn by yet another person. As John Picton and John Mack describe in *African Textiles*, the production of these gowns may have served to unify the different emirates of northern Nigeria, after the holy wars of the early nineteenth century.

Some exchange of skills took place among neighbouring villages and peoples. The Hausa men, for example, now cast modern Asante gold weights near Kumasi (in Ghana). Therefore it is sometimes hard to attribute the work to one particular tribe. Jan Vansina in *Art History in Africa* argues that the focus of identity should be on the object and not the institution from which it comes. Wherever possible the name of the artist should be recorded, together with the date the object was made, the village or workshop it was made in, and the method by which it was produced.

Grouping objects according to function is problematic in that the piece may serve more than one function or its function may be unclear. Instead Margaret Trowell in her book *African Design* groups items according to the material they are made from, for example wood, metal, ivory and textiles.

The Beginnings of African Art

The earliest known form of art in Africa is rock painting, drawn by the nomadic people of southern Africa and the Sahara. Of those paintings which still survive today, some of the earliest have been excavated in Namibia, in strata of between 19,000 and 26,000 years old. The paintings are on portable pebbles and stones and are depictions of rhinoceros and half-human, half-animal forms. Surviving paintings and engravings on rock shelters are younger but more difficult to date accurately. Some probably date from the late Stone Age, about 10,000 BC. These paintings show people dancing, skinning animals, medicine men performing rituals, animals being hunted, hands, bows and arrows and geometric patterns.

The earliest African sculpture comes from Nigeria, dating from 700–500 BC onwards. This is the famous 'Nok' sculpture, terracotta human and animal figures excavated from the tin mines near the village of Nok. The figures are extraordinary for they display a highly developed artistic tradition produced at a time when long distance trade routes and the sophisticated kingdoms in Ghana had barely been established.

There is archaeological evidence that metallurgy existed as early as 3000 BC in northern Africa, from where it spread to Mauritania. There are no works of art in metal surviving from these early periods, although we know that by 700 BC iron smelting had reached Nigeria and by 500 BC iron was worked in Ethiopia and the Great Lakes area of East Africa. Much later the kingdoms of Ife and Benin in Nigeria became important bronze-working centres (although many of the items described as bronze are in fact brass). The majority of bronze heads and figures excavated from Ife (the ritual centre of the Yoruba people) were probably made during the fourteenth century, whilst casting in Benin seems to have flourished during the sixteenth and seventeenth centuries (see **66–69** for examples of cast Benin bronzes). Beads were an important trade item for the people of Ife and many of the bronzes show people wearing beads and bead head-dresses similar to the ones worn by the Yoruba chiefs today (see **25**). However, from the sixteenth century, the power of Ife seems to have declined, as the neighbouring states of Benin and Oyo expanded and took over trade routes. In the nineteenth century Ife was destroyed by the campaigns of Oyo and all traditions of metal casting ended with it.

The Patterns

Designs on bodies, jewellery, clothes and houses all help to establish personal and communal identity, and signs and symbols have special meaning for members of specific communities. In African art there is a tendency to distort natural forms for the purpose of emphasising certain characteristics, and with the application of symbolic motifs, this leads to a predominance of geometric forms. Variations of different geometric shapes and patterns recur throughout African art, and probably reach their summit in Islamic designs (see **5–8**). Islamic patterns provide a good example of the way in which patterns are created in an attempt to interpret and express the world around us. Underlying all Islamic design is the need to express the unity of Allah. That unity holds together the diversity and multiplicity of the world, and this relationship is expressed no better than in the complex interlocking patterns (seen, for example, on **8**). Islamic design can be reconstructed mathematically using a grid of circles, squares and triangles (see *Islamic Designs* by Eva Wilson in this series).

There may be various reasons why an object is patterned. The pattern may serve a function, for example to preserve the walls of a house, or it may enhance the status of the owner or the artist, as in some of the highly decorated Kuba vessels. Alternatively, the patterns may be purely decorative, enhancing the overall design or framing an image.

The Yoruba carved wooden doors are often made up of a series of scenes, each one framed or separated from the next by a linear lattice-work pattern (as on **32**). These borders are called *eleyofo* in Yoruba and they serve to organise the scenes into a narrative order. The door panels are significant as, unlike most African sculpture, they describe events which took place over a period of time.

Designs on buildings can help preserve the structure. The sculptured mud around Hausa doorways strengthens the edges, and Ndbele murals in southern Africa add a protective layer of paint to the mud walls. The designs also have symbolic meaning. Some of the Ndbele designs are 'architectural', enhancing the structure of the dwelling and depicting steps, verandas and doors (97).

Specific motifs may have a name and the Kuba have over two hundred named patterns. Sometimes the name given reflects the shape of the pattern which may have a similarity to something in real life, like the track of an iguana. In other cases it might be named after the person who designed it, but more often than not the name will have no meaning that we can discover. The Kuba are extraordinary in their desire to decorate absolutely everything – cooking utensils, furniture, houses, their own bodies, textiles and clothes. John Picton and John Mack in *African Textiles* discuss Kuba embroidery and describe how new patterns are continually being created. A variation in a textile design may be worked on, and only when it is satisfactorily different will it be given a new name.

Sometimes patterns or motifs are symbolic. Fante flags (see 35) have proverbial meanings and can represent historic events. They were used in warfare to communicate provocative messages or to celebrate victory. A flag bearing the image of a vulture meant 'we came to fight but not you, mere vultures'.

In north Africa, belief in the power of the 'evil eye' to cause harm existed before the arrival of Islam but it was fostered by the words of the Koran which warn against the 'envious person'. Thus, as John Mack and Christopher Spring describe, many of the motifs in textiles and on objects serve to deflect or harm the evil eye. For example, the hand with five straightened fingers (5) can pierce the evil eye, and so can the two knives 'aska biyu' and the eight knives 'aska takwas' on the embroidered pockets of the Hausa gowns (24).

Symbolism in Benin art has been studied in detail, in particular in a book edited by Paula Ben-Amos and Arnold Rubin called *The Art of Power, the Power of Art*. The crocodile (66 and 67), the fish-eagle (65), the python (59) and the elephant (70) are all emblems of legitimate authority. The crocodile eating a fish (66) symbolised the ruler exerting authority over the ruled. The hand is a symbol of what can be achieved through personal effort, rather than what is bestowed by destiny.

Although the drawings in this book are in black and white, colour plays an important part in the symbolism of African art. In Benin, the red coral beads and the red cloth worn by the king issue a threat to his enemies. White is associated with the tranquil nature of the gods, in particular the god of the sea. In Ghanaian art, red is worn to show sorrow or dissatisfaction; indigo blue is for womanhood and tenderness; gold is for the wealth of the land and green is for productiveness. Similarly, materials are significant in Benin art. Ivory is only worn by the king and brass by the king and chiefs.

Animals in Art

Perhaps the most striking feature of African art is how often animals are portrayed, both figuratively and stylistically. Often the most geometric of designs is interpreted as being of animal origin, such as the lozenge shape on skirts from Zaire which is said to be a stylised representation of the monitor lizard (84). Creation myths throughout Africa explain the origin of life through the action of animals. For the Yoruba (in Nigeria) the earth took shape when a hen scratched it up from the primordial water, and a chameleon came to inspect it. For the Bambara (in Mali), knowledge of agriculture was imparted by the antelope (see 56–8) and for the Dogon (also in Mali), birds, hyenas and monkeys evict spirits of the dead from the village. Hierarchies within societies echo hierarchies within the animal kingdom. Lions, leopards and elephants are associated with kings and chiefs. In Benin, the king (Oba) and the leopard had a metaphorical relationship; the leopard was king of the wild (nature) and the Oba king of the home (culture). As described by Paula Ben Amos in *The Art of Power, the Power of Art*, the leopard motif is an emblem of authority and symbolises the Oba's right to take the life of another human being.

Modern Design

In many parts of Africa traditional techniques are dying out, but there are still contemporary artists who are developing new initiatives and ideas and are trying to keep the arts alive. The Ghanaian artist Atta Kwami describes how new signs and symbols are continually being developed in Ghanaian art, in particular new symbols on *adinkra* stamps and mural paintings. The artist Akanvoli Abopadongo painted a wall in Sherigu in Ghana in 1990 and called one of the patterns 'Kuyana 'ni dole bobiga', which translates as 'a well-known man who owns different shapes of cows'. Akanvoli describes how she got the idea for the motif by watching herds of cattle from the top of her house, and the shape she designed represents a bird's-eye view.

The Fulani weavers now produce fewer of the prized *kerka* but instead those who spend time in the cities are weaving colourful textiles with machine-spun cottons, which are in high demand from the Malians and tourists. Throughout Africa, where machine-spun yarn is accessible and easy to work with, weavers are producing more cloths and inventing more designs.

Many textile designs in Africa were taken from early European print cottons, which themselves were often copies of Indonesian batik. In Nairobi batik now proliferates, an example of the localisation of an imported craft, using imported materials and styles.

Missionaries have in many places encouraged the continuation of traditional art forms. In Ghana the Catholic Church has commissioned several artists to decorate church walls. There have also been specific programmes set up, funded by the government, to support indigenous crafts. In Botswana, Design and Development Services is just one organisation which promotes the work of basket-makers. Since baskets do not last for very long and as they were beginning to be replaced in the whole of southern Africa by plastic bowls and utensils, many of the designs and patterns were dying out. But since the 1970s, baskets have been much more widely appreciated by art collectors, tourists and people living in Botswana, and the styles and designs have survived, with many new ones being created. Beth Terry, who works for Design and Development Services, describes in her article on the weavers how there are now many more women weaving baskets in southern Africa than ever before. Weaving is now the only source of income for ninety per cent of weavers, compared with twenty per cent in 1970. The traditional forms have been developed and changed to suit the needs of western homes, for example the traditional round winnowing basket has been made square to form a tray. The grinding mat is sold as a table mat and smaller ones are made for drinks coasters. Sleeping mats are now made for floors in Safari lodges, and storage baskets are made into very popular laundry baskets. In Lesotho pointed woven hats have been made into lids for baskets.

In the early 1970s in Botswana and Zimbabwe, there were virtually no designs on baskets, or they were very limited, evolving out of the weaving technique itself. The baskets were made in the natural colour of the palm. But in the late 1970s and early 1980s designs began to be developed and were given names such as 'swallow tail' or 'back of a python', and many weavers are receiving lessons in colour combination and dying techniques. The weavers themselves are not particularly interested in the naming of patterns. It is mainly the sellers and commercial buyers who develop the names as a marketing strategy.

New patterns and techniques have also been developed in South Africa by the Zulu basket-makers, who now make the colourful *imbenge* telephone wire baskets. These play an important part in the exchange of gifts at Zulu weddings. The men once made baskets out of woven grass but as rural people moved to the cities, they made them out of anything that was available. Now they buy telephone wires especially, the colour of the basket depending on availability of the wires.

Marketable crafts all over Africa have been influenced by European artists and the demands of the commercial market. The basket weaving programmes in southern Africa are just one example. In other places there are similar movements, for example the work with stone sculptors in Zimbabwe. In Egypt tent-makers, whilst continuing their traditional work, are now making appliqué cushion covers and bedspreads and producing machine-printed copies of appliqué wall hangings. African design continues to develop, making it even more important to record those patterns and techniques which are changing or falling out of use.

Notes on the Designs

Unless otherwise stated, all the registration numbers given are for objects from the Museum of Mankind.

1 Pottery dish. Cream with red and black painted background. The Rif, Morocco. The Kabyles are Berbers living in the Djura Mountains, to the east of Algeria. They are famous for their silver jewellery and the pots they make and decorate. Styles vary between groups within this area. Diameter 18 cm. 1979 AF 1.22.

2 TOP LEFT Pottery dish, Berber area, west of Grande Kabyle. Cream background, red and black pattern. Diameter 23.2 cm. 1979 AF 1.14. TOP RIGHT Dark red pattern on white background, the base of the pot on page 3. Width 21 cm, 1917 12–4.1. BOTTOM Pottery dish with dark red stripes on white (reverse of page 1). Rif, Morocco. Diameter 18 cm, 1979 AF 1.22.

3 TOP Pottery dish, Berber area west of Grande Kabyle, Algeria. Yellow with red and black background. Diameter 18.3 cm, 1979 AF 1.10. CENTRE Painted decoration around the side of a pot. Berber area west of Grand Kabyle, Algeria. Cream background with red and black pattern. Height 11 cm, 1979 AF 1.17. BOTTOM Pattern on the side of the Moroccan pot on page 2 (top right). Dark red on cream. 1917 12–4.1.

4 TOP Part of the painted decoration on a water pot from Tunisia. Cream background with brown pattern. Height 22 cm, width 12.5 cm. 7775. BOTTOM Painted decoration around a pottery vessel. Cream background with red and black patterns. Grand Kabyle, Algeria. Height 15 cm. 1929 11–5.1.

5 Berber silver jewellery from Algeria. From LEFT to RIGHT: TOP ROW Silver pendants from Algeria, the first two drawings showing the fronts, the second two the reverse sides. Length of left-hand pendant 5.2 cm, 4622 and 4623. SECOND ROW The first, second and fourth drawings are silver pendants from Algeria. Diameter of left-hand pendant 5 cm, 4621 and 4620 (front and reverse). The third drawing is the silver part of a necklace made of coral beads and silver chains. Algeria, Kabyle. Length 6.5 cm, 1907 3–16.3. THIRD ROW Silver pendants from Algeria, the second with green and blue enamel inlay. Length of left-hand pendant 5.5 cm, 4624, 4610, 4625, 4626. FOURTH ROW Silver pendant from Algeria. The inverted triangle symbolises the feminine image. Width 37 cm, 1943 AF 14.9. Silver pendant in the shape of a hand. *Khamsa* means 'five' in Arabic. Various other motifs incorporating the number five, for example 'the house of five' (see page 24) are also referred to as *Khamsa* and have a similar symbolic derivation and function. Length 5 cm, 6754. FIFTH ROW Silver engraved pins from Algeria. The first forms part of one of the most common pieces of jewellery, used to hold draped shoulder garments in place. The whole thing consists of a chain, a pendant and a pin at the top which is inserted into the cloth. Length of left-hand pin 9.7 cm. 1943 AF 14.11 and 12, 4617 and 4616.

6 TOP Decoration around the inside of a blue and white pottery glazed bowl from Morocco. Diameter 28.2 cm, 1992 AF 1.60. The BOTTOM drawing shows the decoration on the outside. MIDDLE Decoration around the middle of a Moroccan pottery glazed vessel, mainly white with red, yellow and black patterns. Height 53 cm, 1922 AF 1.21.

7 Two glazed pottery jars, the TOP brown and white from Morocco, height 39 cm, the LOWER blue and white and shown with its lid, height 29 cm. 1922 AF 1.81, 1922 AF 1.28 a and b.

8 Decorations on blue and white Moroccan pottery. TOP LEFT On the centre of a food cover. Width 21 cm, 1992 AF 1.33 a and b. TOP RIGHT On the inside of a tajine for cooking. Diameter 38 cm, 1992 AF 1.70 a and b. BOTTOM On the inside of a bowl. Diameter of left-hand bowl 12.5 cm, 1992 AF 1.50. Right-hand bowl 1922 AF 1.60 (see page 6).

9 TOP Two large pottery dishes from Algeria in earthy red with white patterns. Diameters 40.5 cm, 27 cm, 1974 AF 20.34 and 36. BOTTOM Pottery dish on a stand with three bowls. Wikabylia, Fort National Area, Algeria. Yellow background with black stripes and dots and red centres. Height 20.5 cm, 1944 AF 4.328.

10 TOP ROW, LEFT and RIGHT Silver rings and CENTRE silver amulet (length 17.8 cm) from Ghadamsi, Libya. Diameter of left-hand ring 4.7 cm, 1981 AF 5.16, 25 and 18. BOTTOM ROW Silver brooch from Ghadamsi, Libya. Length 14 cm, 1981 AF 5.19 a and b.

11 TOP LEFT and RIGHT, BOTTOM LEFT An armlet, part of a second armlet opened out, and a third armlet all made from brass, from Ethiopia. Length of top armlet 16 cm, 1866 2–19.1, 1913 6–16.6, 1912 4–10.5. BOTTOM RIGHT Brass buckle on a belt, Ethiopia. Diameter 11 cm.

12 Christianity was given state recognition in Ethiopia around 330 AD with the arrival of a Tyrian missionary, St Frumentius. The Ethiopian cross is based on the form of the Greco-Roman cross and has five types: the neck cross worn by men; the pectoral cross, worn by women; the priest's cross used for benediction; the processional cross carried on a staff; and the church cross displayed on the rooves of all Ethiopian church buildings. Processional crosses have a prominent role in the Ethiopian Orthodox church ceremonies. They are used not only in processions but for blessings at the end of the Holy Service. The processional cross LEFT is brass. Length 36.6 cm. The cross RIGHT is bronze. Length 31.5 cm, 68 12–30.8, 68 10–1.19.

13 TOP RIGHT Simple crosses of this kind were usually made of iron, and in an even more unadorned form. Some are probably among the earliest Ethiopian crosses. Length 30.8 cm. *Museum of the Institute of Ethiopian Studies, Addis Ababa.* BOTTOM Processional cross from Ethiopia. Length 46.8 cm, 68 10–1.16.

14 CENTRE Ethiopian cross. Length 31.5 cm. *Museum of the Institute of Ethiopian Studies, Addis Ababa.* The surrounding motifs come from an Ethiopian manuscript. They decorate the pages and are drawn in ink and coloured in reds, yellows, blues and greens. Width of top drawing *c.*4 cm. *British Library*, OR 481 103 (B).

15 Decorations from Ethiopian manuscripts. TOP Late 17th-century manuscript of the Octaleuch, four gospels and synods, in yellow and red. The rest are pre-20th century and from SECOND to BOTTOM are coloured in yellow, orange and black; black, yellow and red; and white and yellow. *British Library*, OR 481,f 125V, OR 516 f5, OR 507 47, OR 507 115, OR 507 115.

16 TOP LEFT Burnished earth-red pottery foot scraper in the shape of a crocodile, with carved and incised patterns. Length 22 cm, 1937 6–17.5. BOTTOM LEFT Burnished earth-red pottery with carved and incised pattern and a bird on top. The drawing TOP RIGHT is its underside. Length 13 cm, 1937 6–17.7. BOTTOM RIGHT Burnished earth-red pottery foot scraper in the shape of a dog, with incised patterns. Length 12 cm, 1937 6–17.6.

17 External decoration on painted bowls made from cow dung, the TOP and BOTTOM LEFT from Kadaru, Sudan, in brown, black and white. Diameter of top bowl 25 cm. 1936 7–15.49, 1948 AF 6.3. The bowl BOTTOM RIGHT is black and white and was made in the Nuba Mountains, Jebel Kadero (Kadaru), East Sudan. 1936 7–15.50.

18 Throwing knives from Sudan are now largely obsolete as weapons, if indeed that was ever their primary function. The different parts of the weapon are described by the Ingassana in anthropomorphic terms – the blade is the head, the spur is the breasts, the shaft is the loins and the handle is the legs. The

cross-hatched incised patterns on the neck (TOP RIGHT and BOTTOM LEFT) represent the traditional monitor-skin neckband worn by men and women (see chapter by Chris Spring in *Swords and Hilt Weapons*, Weidenfeld and Nicolson, 1989). TOP LEFT Metal blade with leather handle, Wadai, Chad. Length 61 cm, 1938 10–12.1. CENTRE Metal blade with leather-bound handle, Omdurman, Sudan. Length 70 cm, 1936 5–8.8. TOP RIGHT Thowing knife or 'sai' in the form of a stylized snake. Iron blade with engraved motifs with wood and leather handle. Ingassana, Sudan. Length 85.5 cm, 1928 4–9.21. BOTTOM LEFT Throwing knife or 'muder' with a scorpion engraved on the metal blade. Leather handle. Ingassana, Sudan. Length 74 cm, 4388. BOTTOM RIGHT Metal blade with engraved motifs and leather handle. Possibly Nuer, Sudan. Length 66 cm, 1944 AF 7.2.

19 Axes with incised iron blades and wooden handles decorated by scorching and engraving. Hausa, N. Nigeria. TOP ROW Lengths 55 cm, 51.2 cm; 1959 AF 1.11, 1954 AF 23.1254. BOTTOM ROW Lengths 60 cm, 43 cm, 57.5 cm; 1954 AF 23.1259, 1962 AF 17.59, 1954 AF 23.1257.

20 – 21 These images are taken from gourds, very finely engraved with a hot metal point making black lines and dyed with red-ochre colour. The gourds were probably made by a Hausa artist who was brought to England in 1924 to make souvenirs for the British Empire Exhibition in Wembley in that year. The label on one gourd identifies the artist as a Hausa/Fulai man (Audu Mai Alijeta) from the town of Jalingo, located south-west of Zinna in Gongola State, Nigeria (M. C. Berns, *The Essential Gourd. Art and History in Northeastern Nigeria*, California 1986). The pictures show elaborately clothed Hausa men and women, people with painted hair and men on beautifully harnessed horses. The making of horse trappings is one of the most spectacular forms of Hausa art, combining leatherwork, wood carving, metalwork, embroidery and weaving. **20** TOP LEFT, TOP RIGHT and BOTTOM RIGHT and **21** BOTTOM RIGHT Height 21.5 cm, 1954 AF 23.1284. **20** TOP CENTRE Width 9.5 cm, 1954 AF 23.1287. **20** BOTTOM LEFT and **21** TOP LEFT Height 21.5 cm, 1954 AF 23.1283. **20** BOTTOM CENTRE and **21** BOTTOM RIGHT Figure, and motor car based on the British Austin dating from the mid-1920s. Height 17 cm, 1954 AF 23.1285. **20** BOTTOM CENTRE RIGHT and **21** BOTTOM CENTRE Height 25 cm, 1954 AF 23.1282. **21** BOTTOM LEFT Width 9.5 cm, 1954 AF 23.1278.

22 TOP and CENTRE Decorated gourd bowls, engraved and blackened with poker-work, Hausa, Nigeria. Diameters 31 cm, 12.5 cm, 1951 AF 12.132, 1946 AF 18.210 c. BOTTOM Exterior decoration on a gourd bowl, engraved but not blackened. Diameter 32 cm, 1951 AF 12.133.

23 These leather cushions are probably Hausa. They are most often made of goatskin, which is dyed to a bright red colour. The black stain is iron oxide. TOP Part of a leather cushion cover (fringe not shown). The central piece of the cushion is similar in style to the *adire* cloths of the Yoruba, with contrasting squares of repeating patterns (see page 34) in red and black. Nigeria. Length 81 cm, 1950 AF 36.2. BOTTOM LEFT Circular leather cushion cover with fringe. Red and black. Diameter 76 cm, 1950 AF 36.1. BOTTOM RIGHT Circular leather cushion, probably Hausa, Nigeria, embroidered with thin strips of coloured leather and appliqué with pieces of leather. White, black and brown. Diameter 54 cm, 1978 AF 7.13.

24 The TOP two embroidered gowns are composed of four parts: the narrow strip of woven cloth forming the body of the gown; the *linzami*, a triangular piece fitted into the neck in the front; a large embroidered pocket sewn onto the front; and a plaited band which reinforces the material. Each part was probably made by a different craftsman. The motifs are similar to those found throughout N. Africa, and many serve to protect the wearer from the evil eye, such as the *aska takwas* or 'eight knives' which can be seen on the TOP two gowns. The circle (*tambari*) is 'the king's drum'. Other common motifs are the double square, or eight-pointed star (TOP LEFT) and the House of Five (BOTTOM). TOP Cotton indigo-dyed gowns embroidered with silk. Hausa, Nigeria. Lengths 79 cm, 150 cm, 1948 AF 25.9, 1934 3–7.215. BOTTOM Red, white and blue embroidery on a brown cotton gown. West Africa. Length 112 cm. *Beving Collection*, 1934 3–7.218.

25 Beads are worn by those who represent the gods – kings and priests – and those with whom the gods communicate – kings, priests, diviners and doctors. To make the crowns (TOP LEFT) the beads are strung together into strands of single colours and are then tacked onto the surface until it is completely covered. The frame may be of wicker or cardboard. The crown always has three components – a face, a beaded fringed veil, *ibojn*, for state occasions when the king is incarnated with divine powers and it is dangerous to stare at him, and beaded birds which symbolise communication with the gods and spirits. (See 'The Sign of the Divine King' by Robert Farris Thompson in *African Arts*, volume 3 (3), 1970.) TOP LEFT Brightly coloured Yoruba bead crown made with red, yellow, blue, white, green and black beads. There is some evidence that there was considerable mingling of the metal crown-making traditions of the ancient Yoruba and the people of Benin. Length 45 cm, 1954 AF 23.261. TOP

RIGHT Appliqué leather and cloth 'shango' bag. Yoruba. Length 35 cm, 1979 AF 1.3248. BOTTOM LEFT Embroidered blue, red, yellow, white and black beads on a leather and cloth bag. Yoruba. Length 47.5 cm, 1965 AF 2.2. BOTTOM RIGHT A single appliqué square on a Yoruba bag. Brown, blue, red and light tan. Length of bag 64 cm, 1954 AF 23.408.

26 – 27 Brass trays from Efik, S. Nigeria and **26** BOTTOM RIGHT the base of a vessel. Diameter 16 cm, 1936. 11–4.6. **26** TOP ROW Diameter 35 cm, 1963 AF 6.14. Diameter 18 cm, 1963 AF 6.17. BOTTOM LEFT Diameter 15.5 cm, 1963 AF 6.18. **27** TOP as **26** TOP LEFT. CENTRE Diameter 35.5 cm, 1963 AF 6.15.

28 – 29 Wooden fans, Ibibio, S. Nigeria, decorated with poker-work method floral designs. **28** LEFT Length 66.5 cm, 1952 AF 20.141. RIGHT Length 61.5 cm, 1934 3–7.488. **29** TOP ROW Length 58.5 cm, 1934 3–7.485. Length 39 cm, 1952 AF 20.87. CENTRE Length 49 cm, 1934 3–7.486.

30 – 33 Wooden Yoruba door panels, Nigeria. The carving and location of the doors indicated the rank and prestige of the kings, chiefs and wealthy men of Yoruba society. The panels contain narrative scenes, carved in relief and framed by *eleyofo* or decorative borders. The scenes are unusual for African sculptures which tend not to be descriptive (see J. M. Borgatti in *African Arts* volume 3 (1), pp. 14–19). **30** TOP A tortoise and a bird. Height 21 cm. BOTTOM A crocodile eating a mudfish. Height 42 cm. Both 1944 AF 4.80. **31** TOP Two men wrestling. Height 28.5 cm. **32** TOP A man on a bike. Height 41.5 cm. Both 1946 AF 12.5–7. **31** BOTTOM A snake. Height 37.5 cm, 1963 AF 2.1. **32** BOTTOM Row of birds. Height 37 cm, 1903 7–27.2. **33** Two figures with legs in the form of fish. Height 30 cm, 1944 AF 4.80 (see mud fish, page 30). BOTTOM 1950 AF 45.547.

34 Yoruba *adire* cloths, from Nigeria. *Adire* refers to cloths produced by the resist dye technique. The two methods are starch-resist (*adire eleko*) and stitching-resist (*adire oniko*). The patterns shown here are produced by the starch-resist method. Each has a name, either proverbial, or taken from the pattern, such as 'bird'. Commemorative cloths (TOP) often have images of the crowned king to denote an event of importance, in this case *ogun pari*, 'the war has finished' (*African Textiles*, Picton and Mack, 1992). TOP LEFT Stencilled designs. Length 162 cm, 1971 AF 35.26. TOP RIGHT, BOTTOM LEFT and RIGHT Hand-painted patterns from a cloth whose overall pattern is named *Olukun* or 'goddess of the sea'. Length 196 cm, 1971 AF 35.17. TOP CENTRE Stencilled pattern. Width 173 cm, 1971 AF 35.19. BOTTOM CENTRE Stencilled pattern depicting a bird. Yoruba, Ife. Width 180 cm, 1953 AF 17.24.

35 Brightly coloured Fante flags from Ghana, made from appliqué, patchwork and embroidery. The flags identified different Fante warrior groups known as *Asafo*, and were used during warfare to intimidate the enemy (*Asafo! African flags of the Fante*, Adler and Bernard, 1992). TOP LEFT A cock taken from a flag bearing the message 'we control the cock and the clockbird' – we control time and decide when things are to be done. TOP CENTRE This flag could symbolise a historic confrontation, or represent the protection of a sacred lake or pond. The Union Jack dates from the British presence in Ghana, and was replaced after independence by the Ghanaian tricolor. TOP RIGHT Vulture taken from a flag with the proverb 'we came to fight but not you, mere vultures'. The vulture is regarded by the Akan as an unpleasant and offensive bird. CENTRE LEFT The pattern depicts the proverbs 'will you fly or will you vanish' and 'without the head, the snake is nothing but rope'. CENTRE The lion is not found in the forests of the Fante but its popularity as a symbol of power comes from its frequent use in European heraldry. CENTRE RIGHT This beast is inspired by the dragon in European heraldry. BOTTOM The tree of life.

36 Asante brass vessels (*kuduo*), Ghana, made by the lost-wax method: the item is moulded in wax, the clay is put around the wax leaving a hole for the wax to escape, the vessel is heated so that the wax melts and escapes and finally metal is poured into the clay mould. It is decorated during the wax modelling stage. The vessels were highly valued by the Asante and used to carry food and drink offerings to ancestors at special rites. They were sometimes filled with gold dust and buried with people of status. These drawings show less elaborate vessel lids with symbols of locks, leg irons or fetters, bows and arrows and keys. See *The Asante* by M. D. McLeod, 1981. TOP Two combs, two loin-cloths, shackles and a whip. Diameter 10.8 cm, 1978 AF 22.132 a and b. CENTRE The symbols include two loin-cloths. Diameter 10 cm, 1947 AF 13.18 a and b. BOTTOM Rodent eating a snake. Diameter 10 cm, 1978 AF 22.130 a and b.

37 TOP ROW Lids of Asante brass vessels. LEFT for holding gold dust. Length 23 cm, 1938 5–9.1. RIGHT This lid of a brass *kuduo* vessel has a handle attached, not drawn. Diameter 10 cm, 1978 AF 22.178. BOTTOM LEFT and RIGHT Brass *forowa* vessel, Kumasi, Ghana. The designs of Guinea fowl and snakes are punched into the front of the object and filled with white pigment so that the designs stand out. This kind of vessel is made from sheet brass with repoussé work and is used to contain cosmetics. *Forowa* are usually European in style. Height 20 cm, 1936 10–22.7.

38 – 39 Gold was an important part of Asante leaders' regalia. When the Portuguese came to the Gold Coast they described the chiefs as covered in gold trinkets, indicating that gold-casting was well established by the fifteenth century. Gold flowed into the royal court and was traded with the Europeans for weapons, gunpowder and shot, and was used to buy European metalware, cloth and liquor. The gold-casters at Kumasi in the nineteenth century were under royal control and could cast for senior chiefs with the Asantehene's permission. These gold badges were cast by the lost wax method (see 36) and the decoration moulded from wax threads during the casting process. Some decorations are repoussé work, beaten into the gold after it has been cast. **38** TOP Diameter 22 cm, 1925 10–24.1, 19th–20th centuries. BOTTOM Diameter 9.5 cm, 1900 4–27.25, 19th century. **39** TOP Diameter 4.6 cm, 1942 AF 9.1, 19th–20th centuries. BOTTOM LEFT Diameter 6.8 cm, 1900 4–27.26, 19th century. RIGHT Diameter 6.4 cm, 1900 4–27.29, 19th century.

40 – 44 Wooden boxes from Ghana made for Europeans by a carver who was active in the Abetifi area of Kwatu before 1906. **40** TOP The lid of a box (see 43, top). Height 24 cm, 1978 AF 22.218. BOTTOM The side of a box (see 41, bottom). Length 31.5 cm, 1978 AF 22.211. **41** TOP (See 42, centre). Length 29 cm, 1978 AF 22.213. BOTTOM See 40, bottom. **42** TOP Length 34.5 cm, 1978 AF 22.212. CENTRE See 41, top. BOTTOM Lid with coiled snake. Height 18 cm, 1978 AF 22.216. **43** TOP See 40, top. BOTTOM See 42, bottom. **44** TOP Diameter 23 cm. BOTTOM LEFT Diameter 18 cm. RIGHT Diameter 11.5 cm. All 1954 F23 1513–1519, *The Wellcome Collection, Museum of Mankind.*

45 All Asante stools (*nkonnua dwa*) from Ghana have the same basic form – a rectangular base with a central column supporting a rectangular seat – but vary in detail. They are carved from a single piece of wood. Certain styles, for example the leopard and the elephant, were once carved only for the Asantehene, though now there is no royal control over the stools. Royal or chiefs' stools were larger and more elaborate than others and were sometimes inlaid with gold and silver. Stools of major chiefs are still carried in public by the chief's stool bearers (*The Asante*, M. D. McLeod). TOP LEFT Stool in the form of an elephant. Height 42 cm, 1978 AF 22.806. TOP RIGHT Stool in the form of a leopard, Asante/Fante. Height 49 cm, 1954 +23.3216. BOTTOM LEFT Height 39 cm, 1978 AF 22.808. BOTTOM RIGHT Asante/Fante. Height 33 cm, 1954 +23.3213.

46 – 48 Asante combs from the Barclay collection, Museum of Mankind, collected before the 1920s. **46** TOP Length 19.5 cm, 1978 AF 22.233. RIGHT Length

26.6 cm, 1978 AF 22. 234. CENTRE Length 24 cm, 1948 AF 25.30. **47** TOP Reverse of 46, centre. BOTTOM LEFT Length 22.6 cm, 1978 AF 22.236. RIGHT Length 22.5 cm, 1978 AF 22.235. **48** TOP ROW Length 23.3 cm, 1978 AF 22.237. BOTTOM Reverse of 47, right.

49 *Adinkra* cloth takes its name from the dye used, and means 'goodbye' or 'farewell'. The cloth is likely to have been worn originally at funerals or functions for departing guests, but is now worn at other important occasions. Approximate height of each *adinkra* stamp 5 cm, 1978 AF 22.4 a-r. *Barclay Collection, Museum of Mankind*.

50 – 51 Abbia is a game of chance, like throwing dice. The stones (*mvia*) were carved in relief from the hard, elliptically shaped pips of a tree. The carving serves no purpose in the game and is merely ornamental ('Abbia Stones' by F. Quinn in *African Arts*, volume 4 (4)). The stones are from Yaunde, Cameroon, possibly made by the M'velle people but used by others in Yaunde and Gabon, and from the Beti tribe near Douala, Coastal Cameroon. Length approximately 3 cm, 1948 AF 7-5.58, 1974 AF 2.2 a-am.

52 Cotton caps. TOP ROW Embroidered caps from Sierra Leone, on the LEFT in red and black. Height 39 cm, 2799. RIGHT Height 33 cm, 1943 AF 2.8. BOTTOM ROW Top views of white cotton caps with black embroidery, possibly from Senegal or The Gambia. Height 13.5 cm, 1934 3-7.468. Height 14 cm, 1934 3-7.474. Height 14 cm, 1934 3-7.466.

53 TOP Leather cushion engraved and dyed with a red and black design, from Mauritania. Length 53 cm, 1979 AF 1.562. BOTTOM Leather bag, possibly a water bottle, with red and black design, from Mauretania. Length 85 cm, 1979 AF 1.461.

54 It is thought that when the Portuguese came to the Guinea coast they brought with them Hispano-Moorish textiles and trained the local weavers to copy the patterns. CENTRE LEFT and BOTTOM LEFT are examples of these Renaissance-style geometric patterns which are still woven today. The weavers still incorporate new designs, with faces and people (*African Textiles*, Picton and Mack, 1992). These textiles are from Manjaka or Papel, Guinea Bissau. TOP Black and white cotton with a portrait and name of the revolutionary leader Amicar Cabral. Length 180 cm, 1989 AF 5.164. The remaining drawings are of black-and-white woven cotton textiles which may be used as shrouds to wrap the dead, or worn on special occasions by high-ranking men and women. CENTRE LEFT Length 179 cm, 1989 AF 5.156. CENTRE RIGHT and BOTTOM RIGHT Length 206 cm, 1934 3-7.196. BOTTOM LEFT Length 189 cm, 1989 AF 5.165.

55 These cloths (*bogolanfini*) made by the Bambara, Mali, are made in the discharge-dying method by painting river mud patterns onto yellow-dyed cotton. The dye is discharged from the remaining lighter area using a caustic substance. The remaining cloth is dark brown and off-white. The cloth is made into sleeveless smocks for men, hunters' skirts and women's wrappers, and all the designs have names. TOP Length 134 cm, 1987 AF 7.15. CENTRE Length 147 cm, 1987 AF 7.13. BOTTOM Length 149 cm, 1987 AF 7.11.

56 – 58 The Bambara (or Bamana) are an agrarian people who maintain an elaborate system of sculptural symbols to provide health, growth and prosperity for their crops, animals and people. *Tji wara koun* means, literally, 'farming animal hat' and represents the mythical antelope who taught agriculture to man. Its spirit is evoked during planting and harvest to ensure fertile crops. The headpieces are worn in male and female pairs on basketry caps. The more abstract designs, such as **56** TOP CENTRE, are from Bougouni district. The female always has a baby (e.g. **57** TOP CENTRE). Length of top left drawing 112 cm. All examples are from *Bambara Sculpture from the Western Sudan* by R. Goldwater, Museum of Primitive Art, New York, 1960, except **57** TOP LEFT and CENTRE (1956 AF 27.7 and 8).

For references for objects on pages **59–77** see *The Art of Power, the Power of Art. Studies in Benin Iconography*. Edited by P. Ben-Amos and A. Rubin, 1983.

59 Carvings from two Benin wooden lids. Diameter 31.2 cm, 1954 AF 23.303. Diameter 32.5 cm, 1954 AF 23.304. TOP ROW Face and snake. CENTRE Leopard. BOTTOM Fish and crocodile. The python was king of the snakes and messenger of *Olokun*, lord of the great waters. The crocodile has been mistaken for a horse by scholars.

60 TOP and BOTTOM, and **61** TOP The sides and end of a metal arm rest used by the Oba of Benin. Depth of end 34 cm, 1954 AF 23.403. **60** CENTRE Benin metal armlet with two Portuguese soldiers. Height 14.3 cm, 1944 AF 4.23. **61** Brass bell from the Forcados river, S. Nigeria. The specific date of the bell is unknown, but it is from the period of the Lower Niger Bronze Industry. Height 16.5 cm, 1909 8–11.2.

62 TOP Benin bronze costume mask in the shape of a leopard's head. These masks or pendants were worn, hanging from the left hip, by Edo chiefs. The mask would have had tiny bells hanging from it. The leopard was seen as king of the bush and could be sacrificed only by the king during the annual ceremony to reaffirm his divinity. Height 18 cm, 1954 AF 23.286. BOTTOM Benin leopard made of sheet brass.

Height 11 cm, 1954 AF 21.1.

63 – 65 Benin court wood carvings. Wood was carved by two distinct groups. The wood and ivory guild carved traditional subjects; the royal pages carved only in wood, making stools and miscellaneous objects often showing European influence. **63** TOP and BOTTOM and **64** BOTTOM Sides of a kola nut box with floral, leaf, bird and interlace designs. Height 5.8 cm, 1954 AF 23.306. **63** MIDDLE Plaque showing, on the right, the Oba's sword bearer (*amada*) carrying the ceremonial sword or *ada*. When the tip is held down it represents homage to the ancestors dwelling in the spirit world. The severed heads denote power. At one time human sacrifice was performed to ensure the successful outcome of ceremonies. Sacrificial blood gave mystical power to objects. The central figure is probably the Oba, with the beaded crown and two long strands of beads. The *amada* is wearing red flannel sewn in scallops imitating the skin of the pangolin or scaly anteater. The pangolin represents protection from danger as it rolls into a ball when threatened. Length 66 cm, 1954 AF 23.300. **64** TOP Box end showing two birds with berries in their beaks. Height 19.5 cm, 1954 AF 23.305. CENTRE ROW and **65** BOTTOM Designs from a circular bowl with lid showing birds, leaves, snakes, berries and nuts. Diameter 28.5 cm, 1954 AF 23.302 a and b. **65** LEFT, CENTRE and RIGHT Designs from the lid of a box. It is likely that the bird is not eating the snake but that the snake is emerging from the bird's mouth, indicating the power of the spirits. The interlaced pattern was a sign of status in Benin. Height 6.8 cm, 1944 AF 4.70 a and b.

66 – 67 Bronze plaques from Benin. Several hundred were taken from the city of Benin when the British went there in 1897. Brass and ivory were the two most important materials for royal art forms because of their durability. TOP The crocodile, after the fish, is the second most common figure on the plaques. It was revered for its ferocity and tenaciousness and represented the power of the Oba. Both the king and crocodile had the power to take life. Width 37 cm, 98.1–15 172. BOTTOM Fish are the most common motifs on the plaques (66 of the known 900), and appear in two types, either with beards seen from above, or without beards seen from the side. Width 18.7 cm, 98 1–15.184. **67** TOP The ceremonial sword, *eben*. When held tip down it represents homage to ancestors. When held in the left hand it is associated with the spirit world, in the right hand pointing up it signifies loyalty to the Oba. Length 37 cm, 98 1–15.177. BOTTOM LEFT In Edo thought the head symbolises survival and accomplishment, or, more rarely, the sacrifice of a crocodile to Olokun, king of the waters. Length 45 cm,

98.1–15 182. BOTTOM RIGHT Two Portuguese heads (see 61, top). Length 45.5 cm, 98.1–15 9.

68 – 69 TOP The seat of a Benin bronze stool showing two mudfish, a fish seen as the messenger of Olokun, god of the waters, because it could live both in water and on land. The species depicted here can give electric shocks and is associated with the divine power of the Oba. Other species represent prosperity, fecundity and peace. Length 37.5 cm, 1923 10–13.1. BOTTOM Mudfish from a Benin plaque. The beards or barbels of the fish represent supernatural power. Length 43 cm, 1908 12–5.4. **69** Benin plaques. TOP Two entwined mudfish with barbels. Length 47 cm, 98 1–15.190. CENTRE and BOTTOM A plaque and one of the fishes. Length 46 cm, 98 1–15.193.

70 – 77 In the past all ivory was controlled in Benin by the Oba, who took one of every pair of elephant tusks. Ivory represented strength and longevity, its colour purity, prosperity and peace. The ivory-carvers' guild was known as the *Igbesanmwan*.
70 – 72 TOP LEFT and RIGHT From the lid of a vessel from Owo, Nigeria. The warrior, left, holds a loop dagger and a bow and arrows. Height 11 cm, 78 11–1.327. On the right a man emerges from a snake's mouth, holding a conch shell. CENTRE From an ivory interlocking armlet, Yoruba, Nigeria. Height 16.8 cm, 1920 11–2.1. **70** BOTTOM ROW, **71**, and **72** BOTTOM From an ivory cup with metal ring and base. A crocodile eating a fish, and an elephant with trunk forming two arms and holding leaves, representing power and royalty. The leaves often symbolise medicine. Carved animals decorate the upper circumference of the cup. Other motifs are monkeys, mudfish, a cock (page 71) and an interwoven pattern (page 72). Height 23.2 cm, 1929.30. **72** TOP Yoruba box, S. Nigeria. Note the similar motifs to the elephant (page 70) and the double bird (page 71). 8801. LEFT Bird from a complete elephant's tusk decorated with birds and people from the Babanki-Bafut area of Cameroon. Height of bird 7.5 cm, 1948 AF 40.5. CENTRE Bird from a decorated Benin tusk. Height 25.5 cm, 1961 AF 9.2. RIGHT Benin armlet with Portuguese faces and ceremonial swords. Height 12.4 cm, 1922 3–13.3.

73 LEFT and RIGHT Carved tusk with gold edged base from Sapi, Sierra Leone. Height of angel 9.5 cm, 1979 AF 1.3156. CENTRE Figure from a salt-cellar. The salt-cellar is in three sections and shows Portuguese adventurers and traders. These 'Afro-Portuguese ivories' are amongst the earliest tourist art from Africa. They were made by the royal ivory carvers of the Benin court and intended for export. Late 15th–early 16th centuries. 78.11–1.48 a, b and c.

74 – 77 Carved tusks and figures from tusks. 74 LEFT and CENTRE from Sette Cama, Gabon. Heights 59 cm and 31 cm, 1904. 11–23.3 and 4. RIGHT From the Kongo people, Zaire. Height 38.5 cm, 1940 AF 11.5. 75 All from Zaire. TOP ROW Man holding a teapot, and a man with walking stick and hat. Both 1904 11–22.3. Seated figure, woman, and man with hat and stick. All 1940 AF 11.5. CENTRE and BOTTOM CENTRE and RIGHT Three men with bent leg, tusk and bag, a fish and a man holding a baby. All 1904 11–22.3. BOTTOM LEFT Man holding bananas. 1904 11–22.4. Average height 6 cm. 76 and 77 TOP LEFT and BOTTOM RIGHT Figures from a tusk from the Lower Congo, Zaire. Height of left-hand figure 14.5 cm, 1954 AF 23.1691. 77 TOP RIGHT and BOTTOM LEFT Height 15.5 cm, 1954 AF 23.1962.

78 TOP LEFT and RIGHT, BOTTOM CENTRE Decorated gourds from Zaire. Height 46 cm, 1954 AF 23.1736; 29 cm, 1954 AF 23.1738; 30 cm, 1954 AF 23.1739. The remaining drawings are from a burnished earthenware pot with incised patterns. Height 30 cm, 1954 AF 23.5152.

79 Knives, from LEFT to RIGHT Metal blade and wooden handle from Monzombo, Central African Republic. +5718. Leather-bound handle with decorated metal blade from Yakoma, N. Zaire. 1947 AF 27.4. Copper band handle and metal blade, again from Yakoma. 1949 AF 46.802. Knife with wooden handle and metal blade from N. E. Zaire. 98–158. Knife with a copper-bound handle with metal studs from Ngombe, N. W. Zaire. 1956 AF 12.1. Wooden-handled knife from Cibaya, Cameroon/Central African Republic. 1900 5–25.2. Length of left-hand knife 43.5 cm. MIDDLE ROW Knife and throwing knife from Zaire. Length of left-hand knife 57.5 cm, 1949 AF 46.526, 1947 AF 27.6. BOTTOM ROW, LEFT Sabre knife with engraved lines on the blade, Azande, N. E. Zaire. Height 69 cm, 1979 AF 1.1695. CENTRE Throwing knife from Ngombe, N.W. Zaire. 1947 AF 27.5. Sword from Ngombe. 1979 AF 1.1694.

80 Kuba cut-pile textiles from Zaire. Threads of raffia are pulled through the weave of the textile, leaving a small loose end cut to form a tuft. The result is 'Kasai velvet'. TOP Raffia textile embellished with cut-pile and conventional embroidery in subtle pink with cream, black and grey. The Kuba dye the base-cloth purple and only partly cover the surface with pile so that the dyed sections show through as part of the pattern. Length 72 cm, 1979 AF 1.3210. CENTRE Kuba-Shoowa raffia textile with cut-pile embroidery from Zaire, 19th–20th centuries. The Shoowa cover the whole textile with cut-pile, contrasting dark and light colours, in this case black and natural raffia. Length 71 cm, 1922 3–6.1. BOTTOM The central Kuba peoples use a variety of decorative techniques including conventional embroidery. Kuba-Bushoong, Zaire. Length 65 cm, 1909 5–13.410.

81 Carved wooden boxes made by the Kuba, the Ngongo and Ngeende. They are made by men and used by women to store jewellery and cosmetics. The crescent moon represents the period of highest fertility. TOP THREE Heights 8.87 cm, 7.8 cm, 9.5 cm, 1908 Ty 18, 23 and 33. BOTTOM Length 28 cm, 1909 5–13.33.

82 Drinking cups from Wongo, Zaire. Height of top cup 16 cm. Clockwise from TOP 1910 4–20.11, 49, 29.

83 These woven mats from what is now Zaire were collected before 1928 and acquired by the Wellcome Historical Medical Museum. Length 192 cm, 130 cm, 1954 AF 23.3699 and 3703.

84 Border patterns from women's raffia skirts, Mbuun, S. Zaire, 19th–20th centuries. Raffia is the only raw material used in Zairian weaving. Only men weave, and women do the embroidery. From TOP to BOTTOM Dark brown and natural light-tan raffia. Length 99 cm, 1910 4–20.390. Length 86 cm, 1909 12–10.12. Length 115 cm, 1910 4–20.391. Length 113 cm, 1910 4–20.589.

85 Six woven shallow baskets made by the Tutsi people, Rwanda. TOP ROW, LEFT Diameter 14 cm, 1948 AF 8.37. RIGHT 1937 10–6.5. CENTRE ROW, from LEFT to RIGHT 1937 10–6.6, 1948 AF 8.420 and 8.422, 1937 11–5.4. BOTTOM ROW Three Rwanda baskets with lids, from LEFT to RIGHT Height 32 cm, 1948 AF 8.26 a and b, 8.33 a and b, 8.27 a and b. The basket RIGHT was made in the household of the grand chief Kumusini. The weave is known as koboha, the pattern umuras.

86 A basket from Kenya and Luo stools, also Kenyan. TOP Red, black and natural yellow raffia basket. Diameter 28.8 cm, 1922 6–9.3 b. LEFT Large wooden stool decorated with white, blue, red and black beads. Diameter 48.5 cm, 1943 AF 2.4. RIGHT Stool with red, white, blue, green and yellow beads pressed into the wood. Diameter 45 cm, 1943 AF 2.5.

87 Gourds from Kenya decorated in the poker-work method, where a hot point is used to blacken parts of the gourd. TOP Diameter 15.3 cm. CENTRE Diameter 39 cm. BOTTOM Diameter 36.5 cm. Private Collection of Fenella White.

88 Light-weight Kikuyu dance shields or ndome for the Muumgburo dance. They are usually carved by specialists. Boys pass their shields down to younger brothers, who scrape off the new paint and replace the designs (The Southern Kikuyu before 1903, L. S. B. Leakey, vols 1–3, Academic Press 1977). TOP LEFT Red and black on a white background. Length 67 cm, 1931 11–18.61. TOP CENTRE and RIGHT From Akikuyu of

British East Africa, W. S. Routledge and K. Routledge, 1910. CENTRE Red and black on white. Length 62.5 cm, 1921 10–28.12. BOTTOM LEFT The inside and CENTRE the outside of a shield, painted in red, black and white. Length 63.6 cm, 1931 1.11–18.63. BOTTOM RIGHT Red and black on white. Length 63.6 cm, 1947 AF 16.43.

89 Each major centre in Madagascar has its own range of styles and variety of patterns (*Madagascar. Island of the Ancestors* by John Mack, 1986). Patterns are described using a hierarchy of 'letter', 'word' or 'sentence' depending on their complexity. TOP ROW, LEFT Pink, purple, green and yellow woven basket. Height 35 cm, 1984 N14.342. CENTRE Purple, white and green basket. Height 27 cm, 1984 N14.50. RIGHT Woven basket in pink, green and yellow. Height 35 cm, 1984 N14.345. MIDDLE A woven mat with purple designs on natural-coloured raffia. Length 154 cm, 1985 AF 17.222. BOTTOM LEFT and RIGHT Woven baskets in purple, blue, yellow, green and pink. Heights 34.5 cm, 1984 N14.343, 344.

90 TOP LEFT Decorated window panel. Height 59 cm, (159) 68–0D–33 (ZFMN) *Musée d'Art et d'Archeologie, Madagascar*. TOP RIGHT Carved wooden stool. Height 13.5 cm, 1985 N17.55. BOTTOM LEFT Height 15 cm, (157) 64–5–442 (ZFMN), and BOTTOM RIGHT Decorated wooden box with lid. Height 20 cm, (83) 63.10.15 (a, b) (MF). Both *Museum of Madagascar*.

91 Table mats and CENTRE ROW baskets purchased in Harare market, Zimbabwe, in 1992. Height of top left mat 28.8 cm. *Private Collection*.

92 – 93 Carved wooden headrests, Shona, Zimbabwe. **92** Height of first headrest 15.5 cm. TOP ROW 1956 AF 27.282, 1949 AF 46.815. CENTRE ROW 1935 7–15.5, 1949 AF 46.809. BOTTOM ROW 1935 7–15.1, 1949 AF 46.808. **93** TOP ROW 1921 6–16.43, 1899 4–22.1. CENTRE ROW 1949 AF 46.807, 1952 AF 26.42. BOTTOM ROW 1892 7–14.152 and 151.

94 Baskets are mostly made by the Hambukushu and Bayeyi who live around the Okovango Delta at Basubiya on the Choke River at Bababirwa in Botswana. Generally, women do the weaving, although men make slatted winnowing baskets and huge grain-storage containers. A national and international commercial market has been set up over the last twenty years, reviving the craft throughout Botswana. The designs are each named, often by the sellers rather than the weavers themselves. TOP White printed cotton wall-hanging with a pattern made up of basket designs in black and red, from Mochudi, Botswana. *National Museum, Monuments and Art*

Gallery of Botswana. The designs on the baskets are CENTRE LEFT 'forehead of the zebra' and RIGHT 'shield', BOTTOM LEFT 'urine trail of the bull' and RIGHT 'knees of the tortoise' or 'flight of the swallow'.

95 TOP and CENTRE LEFT Waistbands from South Africa in green, pink, blue, black and white designs. Widths 32 cm, 1949 AF 29.16, 1979 AF 1.2754. RIGHT White, blue, red and black beads. Zulu. Length 42 cm, 1922 11–7.1. BOTTOM Green, white, black and pink with red fringe. Zulu. Width 30 cm, 1937 2–20.2.

96 TOP ROW Bead necklaces and anklets from S. Africa. From LEFT to RIGHT necklace with red and black motifs on a white background, and blue beads for the edge and the tassle, with a coin at the end. Length 52 cm, 1933 6–9.29. Black and white anklet. Length 24 cm, 1910 10–5.30 b. Red and blue motifs on a white background, with a blue, red and white tassle. Length 37 cm, 1933 6–9.21. Black and white anklet. Length 25 cm, 1910 10–5.32 b. Red and black motifs on a white background with blue edging and tassle and a coin at the end. Length 49 cm, 1933 6–9.26. CENTRE ROW from LEFT to RIGHT Black and white anklets. Length of left-hand anklet 18.5 cm. 1910 10–5.31 b, 30 a, 31 a. BOTTOM ROW Xhosa beadwork tie, mainly white with blue and red motifs. Length 33 cm, 1970 AF 24.5. Xhosa necklace, mainly white with red and blue motifs. Length 20 cm, 1970 AF 24.7. White background with red, blue and black motifs. Length 45 cm, 1933 6–9.31.

97 – 100 All drawings are taken from *The African Mural* by P. Changuion, Struik Publishers, Cape Town, 1989. **97** Often the Ndbele artist paints these designs using both hands to form a mirror image. The design BOTTOM LEFT is symmetrical, and those TOP RIGHT and BOTTOM LEFT show rotational symmetry. The latter was painted by Malvel Dasi, an artist from the Orange Free State. Murals are not only intended to preserve the walls of houses, but are also decorative and symbolic (Kwami, 1993). As paintings show wear-and-tear quickly there are few examples of more than three or four years old. Often an artist will paint over the same wall year after year. Ndbele paintings are characterised by three phases, the first using mono-chrome designs, the second depicting stylized plants and animals in colour, the third coloured designs based on modern urban architecture. **98 – 100** Southern Sotho mural paintings have been influenced by Ndbele artists, who use basic geometric forms in their fine beadwork necklaces, armbands, aprons and anklets. Pebbles are used to make mosaic patterns and repeat patterns are created using cardboard stencils.

Further Reading

Aafjes-Sinnadurin, U., *The Kingdom of Benin* (Teachers' Pack). Commonwealth Institute, 1992

Adler, P. and Barnard, N., *Asafo! African Flags of the Fante*, Thames and Hudson, 1992

Bassani, E. and Fagg, W., *Africa and the Renaissance, Art in Ivory*, edited by Susan Vogel. The Centre for African Art, New York, 1988

Ben-Amos, P. and Rubin, A., eds, *The Art of Power, The Power of Art. Studies in Benin Iconography*. The Museum of Cultural History, California, Pamphlet Series 19, 1983

Berns, M., *The Essential Gourd. Art and History in Northeastern Nigeria*. University of California, 1986

Borgatti, J. M., 'Yoruba Doors'. *African Arts* Vol 3 (1), 1969

Brain, R., *Art and Society in Africa*, Longman Group Ltd, 1980

Bravmann, R. A., *Islam and Tribal Art in West Africa*, Cambridge University Press, 1974

Changuin, P., *The African Mural*. Struik Publishers, Cape Town, 1989

Coe, M. D., Connolly, P., Harding, A., Harris, V., LaRocca, D. J., Richardson, T., North, A., Spring, C., and Wilkinson, F., *Swords and Hilt Weapons*. Weidenfeld and Nicolson, London, 1989

Crowe, D. W., 'Geometric Symmetries in African Art', in *Africa Counts* by C. Zaslavsky

Crowley, D. J., *The Crafts as Communication: the Visual Dimension of Pan-Africanism*. University of California, 1979

Davis, C. B., *The Animal Motif in Bamana Art*. The Davis Gallery (catalogue), 1981

Denyer, S., *African Traditional Architecture*, Heinemann Educational Books, 1982

Ellert, H., *The Material Culture of Zimbabwe*, Longman Zimbabwe Ltd, 1984

Fagg, W. and Picton, J., *The Potter's Art in Africa*, British Museum Publications Ltd, 1970

Feest, C., 'European Collecting of American Indian Artefacts and Art', in *Journal of the History of Collections*, Vol 5 No 1, 1993

Garlake, P., *The Kingdoms of Africa*, Elsevier-Phaidon, 1978

Garlake, P., *The Painted Caves. An Introduction to the Prehistoric Art of Zimbabwe*. Modus Publications, Zimbabwe, 1987

Heathcote, D., *The Arts of the Hausa*, World of Islam Festival Publishing Company Ltd, 1976

Jefferson, L. E., *The Decorative Arts of Africa*. Collins, London, 1974

Kwami, Atta, *Signs and Symbols of Ghanaian Painting 1993*. (Unpublished teachers' notes. Copies available from The Commonwealth Institute, London)

Leakey, L. S. B., *The Southern Kikuyu before 1903* Vols 1–3. Academic Press, 1977

Mack, J., *Madagascar. Island of the Ancestors*, British Museum Publications Ltd, 1986

Mack, J., *Emil Torday and the Art of the Congo 1900–1909*, British Museum Publications Ltd, 1992

Mack, J. and Spring, C., *African Textiles*, The National Museum of Modern Art, Kyoto, Japan, 1991

McLeod, M. D., *The Asante*, British Museum Publications Ltd, 1981

Moore, E., *Ethiopian Processional Crosses*, Ethiopia, 1969

Picton, J. and Mack, J., *African Textiles*, British Museum Publications, 1989

Quinn, F., 'Abbia Stones'. *African Arts* Vol 4 (4), 1971

Ross, D. H. and Garrard, T. F., *Akan Transformations. Problems in Ghanaian Art History*, University of California, 1983

Rubin, W. (ed.), *'Primitivism' in 20th Century Art*, The Museum of Modern Art, 1985

Sieber, R., *African Furniture and Household Objects*, Indiana University Press, 1980

Spring, C., 'African Hilt Weapons', in *Swords and Hilt Weapons*, Weidenfeld and Nicolson Ltd, 1989

Terry, M. E. and Cunningham, A. B., 'The Impact of Commercial Marketing on the Basketry of Southern Africa', *Journal of Museum Ethnography*, 1993

The Christian Orient, British Library (catalogue), 1978

Thompson, R. F., 'The Sign of the Divine King. An essay on Yoruba bead-embroidered crowns with veil and bird decorations', *African Arts* Vol 3 (3), Spring 1970

Trowell, M., *African Design*, Faber and Faber Ltd, 1960

Vansina, J., *Art History in Africa*, Longman Group Ltd, 1984

Waljee, A. and Mawji, A., *Design and Technology from an Islamic Perspective* (Teachers' Pack). Commonwealth Institute, 1992

Wilson, E., *Islamic Designs*, British Museum Publications, 1989

Zaslavsky, C., *Africa Counts*, Lawrence Hill & Company, USA, 1979

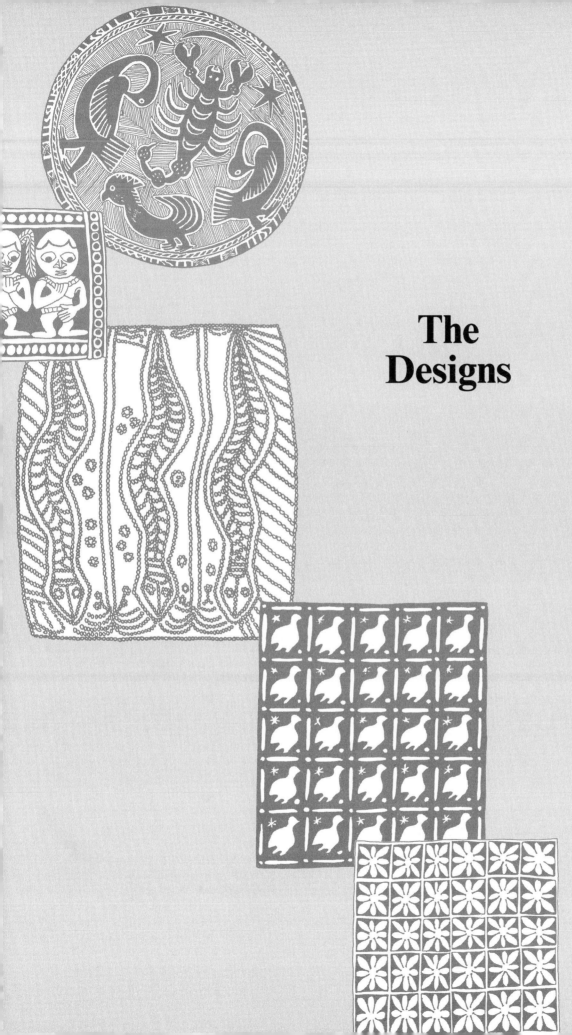

The Designs

Unless otherwise stated, all objects drawn are made in the 20th century.

1 A finely decorated pottery dish from The Rif, Morocco. The background colour is cream, and the pattern is painted in a dark earthy red.

2 Painted dishes from Algeria and Morocco.

3 Painted decorations on pots from Algeria and Morocco.

4 The TOP pattern is taken from a finely painted water pot from Tunisia. The pattern
BELOW is typical of Kabyle pottery from Algeria.

5 Berber silver jewellery from Algeria. On the BOTTOM row are pins used to hold garments in place. The Islamic *Khamsa* (meaning 'five') BOTTOM RIGHT is here represented by the 'hand of Fatima'. It stands for the five prayers or five fundamental principles of Islam and protects the wearer from the evil eye.

6 Painted patterns taken from contemporary pottery from Safi, Morocco. The design TOP is the blue and white decoration around the inside rim of a bowl.

7 Contemporary decorated pottery from Morocco. The TOP jar is in brown and white, and is said to imitate Berber patterns. The BOTTOM vessel with a lid is blue and white.

8 Blue and white designs painted on pottery from Morocco.

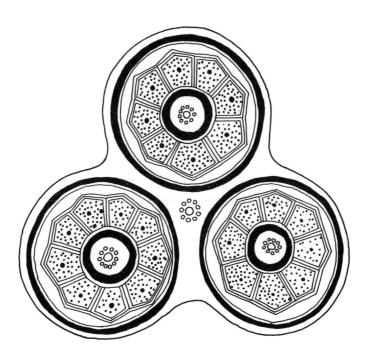

9 Pottery dishes from Algeria. The BOTTOM one has three bowls on a single stem (aerial view).

10 Silver jewellery and an amulet (TOP CENTRE) from Libya. The patterns are embossed and engraved. The two smaller pieces are rings, and the LOWER two are the sides of a brooch.

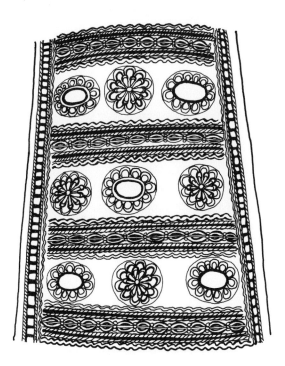

11 Floral designs on a brass buckle (BOTTOM RIGHT) and brass armlets, all from Ethiopia.

12 Two Ethiopian processional crosses, carried by priests of the Ethiopian Orthodox Church during ceremonies. The TOP cross is brass, probably pre-17th century, and the LOWER one is a later bronze cross, probably 17th century, bearing engraved designs of western derivation.

13 A silver 15th-century Ethiopian cross (TOP) from Gojjam decorated with circular finials and engraved birds on the lower arms. BELOW, a bronze 16th-century processional cross from Ethiopia. The interlaced patterns show early Coptic influence. The inscription reads 'this is the cross of our Father, Takla Haymanot'.

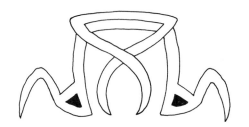

14 A bronze processional cross from Tigre, Ethiopia. 13–14th centuries. Bronze quatre-
foil crosses such as this are probably the most intricate and beautifully made of all
Ethiopian crosses. The surrounding motifs are taken from an Ethiopian manuscript,
probably 18th century.

15 Decorative borders from Ethiopian manuscripts, probably 17th and 18th centuries.

16 Pottery skin-scrapers from Egypt, made in and around Asyut in the late 19th to early 20th centuries, probably for the tourist trade. The TOP RIGHT shows the criss-crossed surface used to rub the skin. BOTTOM LEFT is a side view, TOP LEFT is a view from above, showing the crocodile which forms the handle, and the scraper BOTTOM RIGHT is in the form of a dog.

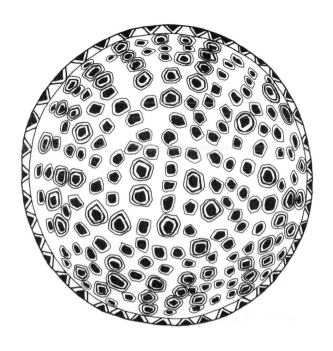

17 These bowls are made from cow-dung and are painted in white, brown and black. From the Kadero Province, Nuba Hills, Sudan.

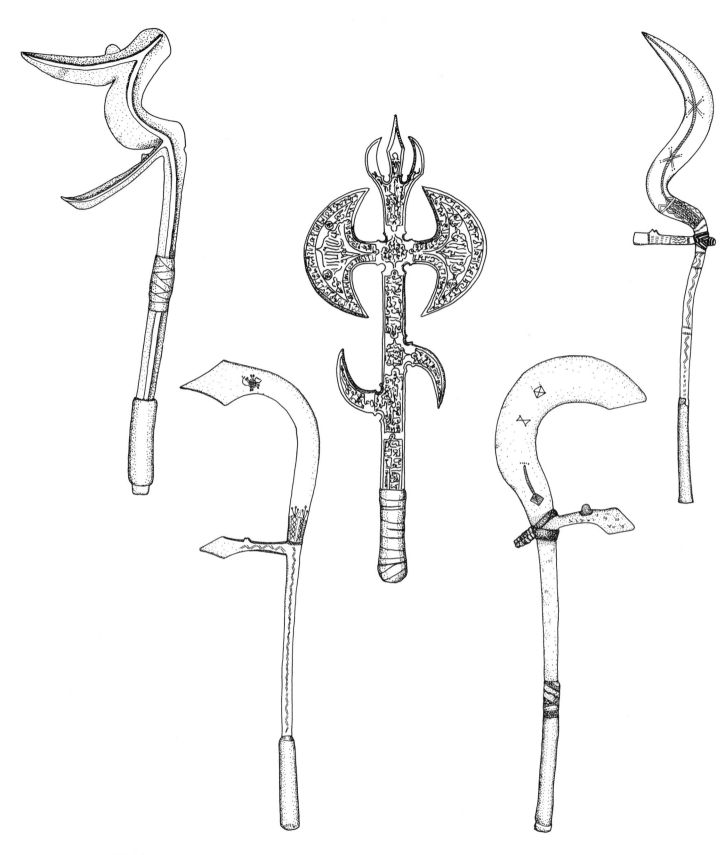

18 Throwing knives and a double-headed axe from Sudan. The central piece is highly decorated with Islamic calligraphy. The entire shape of each weapon forms a spectacular design in itself. The knife TOP RIGHT is in the form of a stylized snake; BOTTOM LEFT has a scorpion engraved near the tip of the blade. The axe CENTRE was probably made during the Madhist period in the Sudan, late 19th century.

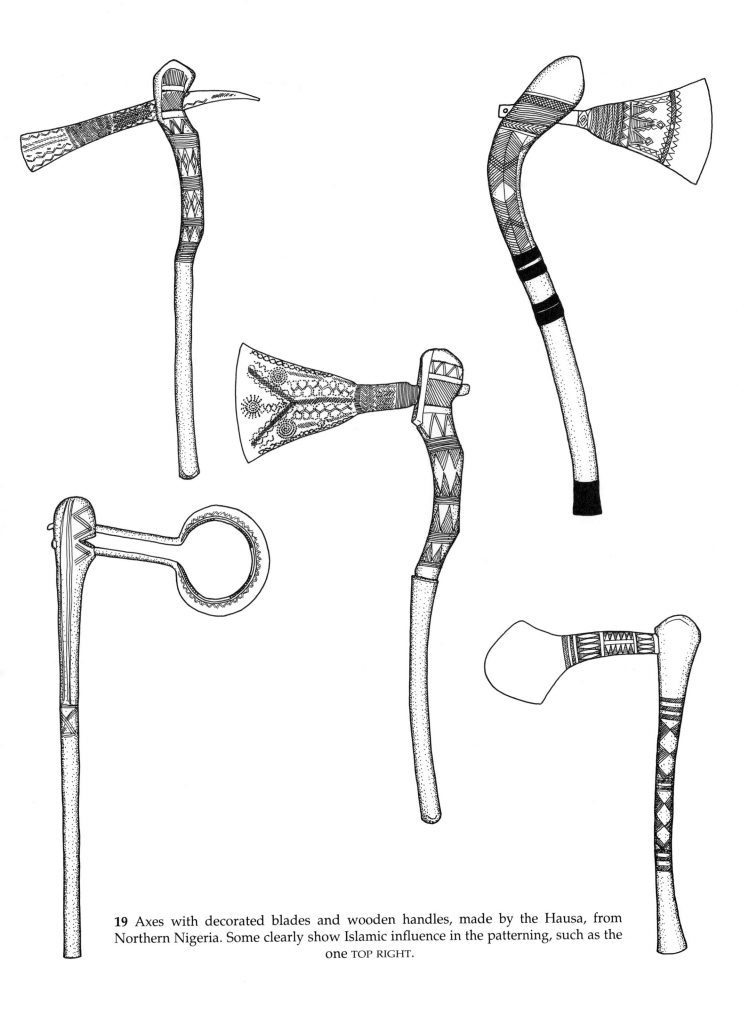

19 Axes with decorated blades and wooden handles, made by the Hausa, from Northern Nigeria. Some clearly show Islamic influence in the patterning, such as the one TOP RIGHT.

20 Zingaru calabash decorated with scenes of warfare and everyday life of the Hausa. Such drawings are unusual in African art and they provide an invaluable record of costume, hairstyles and horse trappings from Northern Nigeria.

21 Decorated calabash from Zingaru, Northern Nigeria. These detailed line drawings are made with a hot metal point which burns thin black lines into the calabash. They record battle scenes, wrestling and a car based on the British Austin dating from 1925.

22 Three calabash bowls, Hausa, Northern Nigeria. The decoration has been carved and engraved onto the outside of the gourd, and in the figures TOP and BOTTOM RIGHT, the pattern has been scorched in parts, giving a striking black-and-white effect.

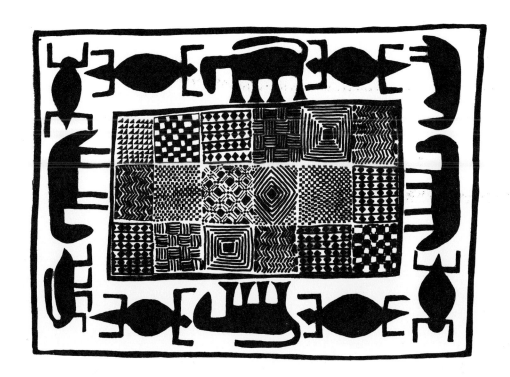

23 Tanned leather cushions decorated with printed geometrical pattern motifs and animal forms (TOP and BOTTOM LEFT) Bida, Nupe, Northern Nigeria. BOTTOM RIGHT Cushion embroidered and appliquéd with pieces of leather, probably Hausa, Northern Nigeria.

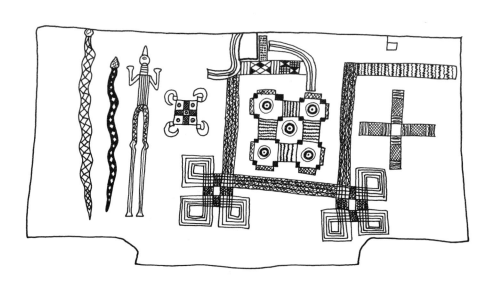

24 These spectacular Hausa embroidered gowns from Northern Nigeria are each made by a number of different craftsmen. The designs on the TOP two gowns both incorporate the *aska takwas*, 'eight knives', and the circular motif to the LEFT of the collar is the *tambari*, 'the king's drum'. The exact provenance of the LOWER one is unknown. It has the Islamic *Khamsa* (meaning 'five') as one of its motifs in the form of the 'house of five'.

25 Examples of Yoruba bead embroidery and appliqué leather bags. TOP LEFT A beaded crown, BOTTOM LEFT a beaded bag. BELOW Decorations on leather bags. The traditional crown always has a beaded fringe to hide the king's face, a beaded bird which symbolises the splendour of communication with the gods, and a frontal beaded face which extends the vision of the king's moral vigilance and wrath.

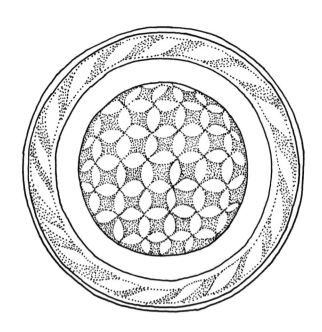

26 Brass trays and the base of a brass vessel (BOTTOM RIGHT) made by the Efik, Southern Nigeria. The punching of the dots to make the pattern gives an added textural quality to the overall design, contrasting smooth and rough surfaces.

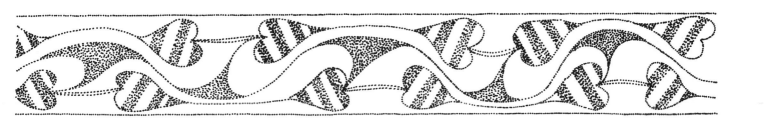

27 BELOW A beautiful beaten brass tray with the floral pattern punched out in dots from the underside, Efik, Southern Nigeria. The TOP design is taken from the plate on page 26 (TOP LEFT).

28 Two wooden fans, Ibibio, Southern Nigeria. The flowing floral designs are characteristic of the work of Eastern Nigeria.

29 Wooden fans, Ibibio, Southern Nigeria. The decorations are made by scorching the lines with a hot metal point, and blackening them with a hot flat implement.

30 These carved wooded Yoruba door panels from Nigeria are fine examples of African architectural sculpture. The carving and location of the doors indicated the rank and prestige of the inhabitant of the dwelling. The TOP panel shows a tortoise and a bird, the LOWER depicts a crocodile eating a mudfish.

31 Two scenes from carved wooden Yoruba door panels, Nigeria. TOP Two men wrestling. BELOW A coiled snake. The narrative aspect of the scenes suggests a European influence introduced into Yoruba culture some time after the 15th century.

32 Two scenes from carved wooden Yoruba door panels, Nigeria. The narrative scenes are carved in relief and framed by a lattice work border pattern called *eleofo*.

33 Sections from two carved wooden Yoruba doors, Nigeria. The doors often portray historic events or scenes of everyday life as well as creating an overall pattern using different borders and frames. The carved angles produce shadows and textures which add to the effect.

34 Designs on indigo starch resist-dyed textiles (a starch paste is applied to the cloth which resists the penetration of the dye). Yoruba, Nigeria. Some are hand-painted, others are created using stencils. These cloths are called *adire* by the Yoruba, and the patterns all have names. TOP A cloth made to commemorate the end of the Nigerian civil war. 'Ogun Pari' means 'war has finished'.

35 The Fante people living in the coastal region of Ghana produced highly coloured appliqué banners and flags used to identify different Asafo military groups. The scenes on the flags carried messages often deliberately to challenge or provoke rival companies. Most flags are decorated with borders of repeating geometric patterns and a white cloth fringe.

36 Lids of three brass *Kuduo* vessels made by the Asante, Ghana. The central piece of each is raised and forms the handle of the lid. The vessels were of great importance to the Asante, and the symbols on them may have signified their usage.

37 Decorations on brass vessels. The TOP two are made by the Asante, Ghana. TOP LEFT has crocodiles in the centre, and the BOTTOM two depict guinea fowl and snakes. These latter two designs are punched into the brass and filled with a white substance.

38 Two gold soul-bearer's discs, Asante, Ghana. These were worn by royal *Kra* servants. They were cast as plain discs with edge decorations made from wax threads and the surface later decorated by repoussé work (beating the metal). 19th–20th centuries.

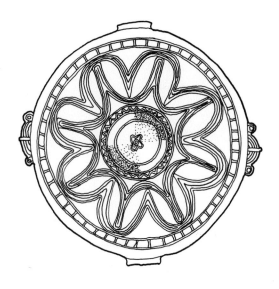

39 The gold badge of the Asante soul-bearer, Ghana. These three examples show very fine workmanship. The circular badge with a motif inside represents the presence and power of God. 19th century.

40 These carved wooden boxes from Ghana, on this page and the following few pages, are early examples of 'tourist art'. The boxes show some traditional motifs, and are elaborately decorated with both geometric designs and animal motifs. The LOWER drawing is of the side of a box, the lid of which is shown on page 41.

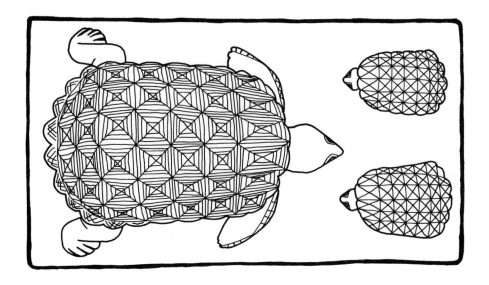

41 Carved wooden boxes from Ghana. These drawings show the lid of two boxes, one with a crocodile eating a fish, and one with three tortoises.

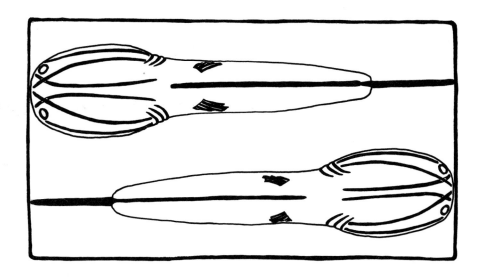

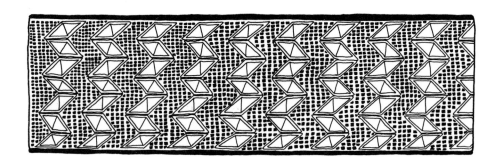

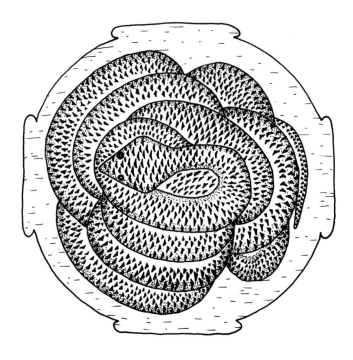

42 Three carved wooden boxes from Ghana. TOP Two mudfish on the lid. MIDDLE The side of a box. BELOW A snake coiled up on a lid.

43 Two carved wooden boxes. The TOP box has intwined snakes running along the side; the LOWER one has geometric designs.

44 Asante calabash bowls from Ghana with very fine engraved patterns of flowers and animals. This technique of decoration leaves large background areas covered with a mass of cross-hatched textured pattern.

45 Carved wooden Asante chieftain stools from Ghana. Many of the stools were designed solely for the Asantehene (chief), and could not be copied without his permission. The elephant and the leopard (TOP two stools) were both such designs.

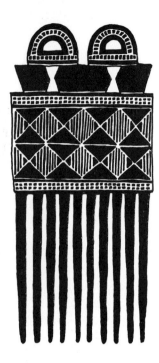

46 Carved wooden combs, Asante, Ghana.

47 Carved wooden Asante combs from Ghana, with carved and engraved patterns.
The central pieces of the combs are chieftain stools (see page 45).

48 Carved wooden Asante combs from Ghana. These drawings show the decoration on the handles; the Asante chieftain stools can clearly be seen in the centre of each (see page 45).

49 Ghanaian *Adinkra* stamps made from calabash and used to print cloth. The various designs of the stamps have different names each with magical, historical or proverbial meaning. TOP LEFT is *Mpuannum* meaning five tufts of hair, a traditional hairstyle, and TOP ROW, third along, is *Msusyidie*, a symbol of sanctity and good fortune. The overall design of *Adinkra* cloth is made up of squares within which individual motifs are repeated.

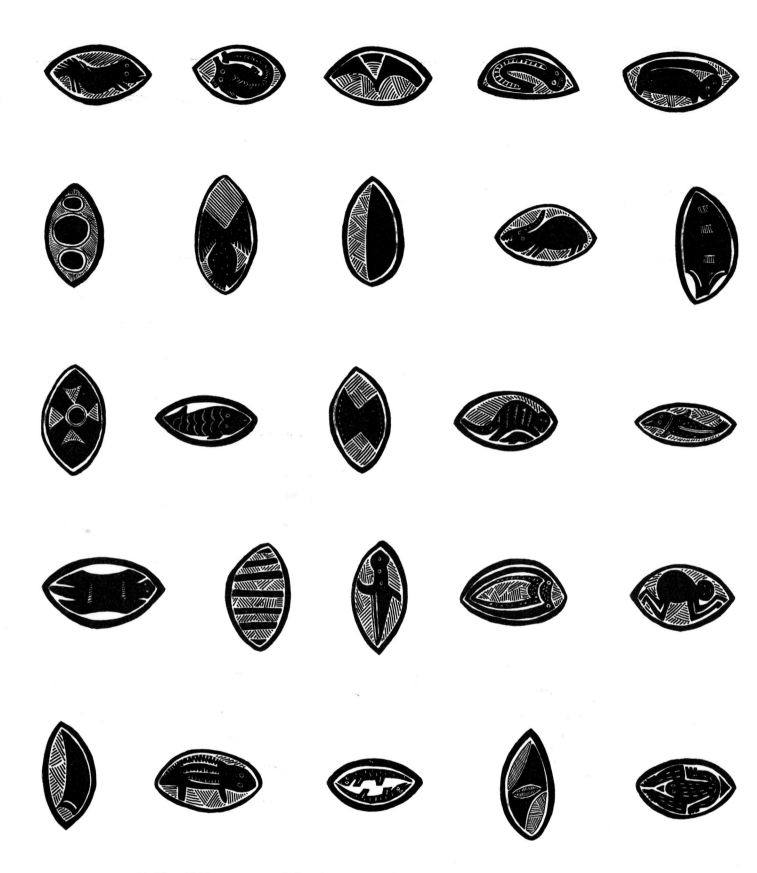

50 The Abbia stones made by the Beti people from Cameroon are a highly decorative form of art. They are carved from the hard pips of the very poisonous fruit of a tree and are used to play the Abbia game. The decorations on each stone appear to be entirely for ornament, as the pictures serve no purpose in the game, but the counters are especially sought for the artistic qualities of the relief carving.

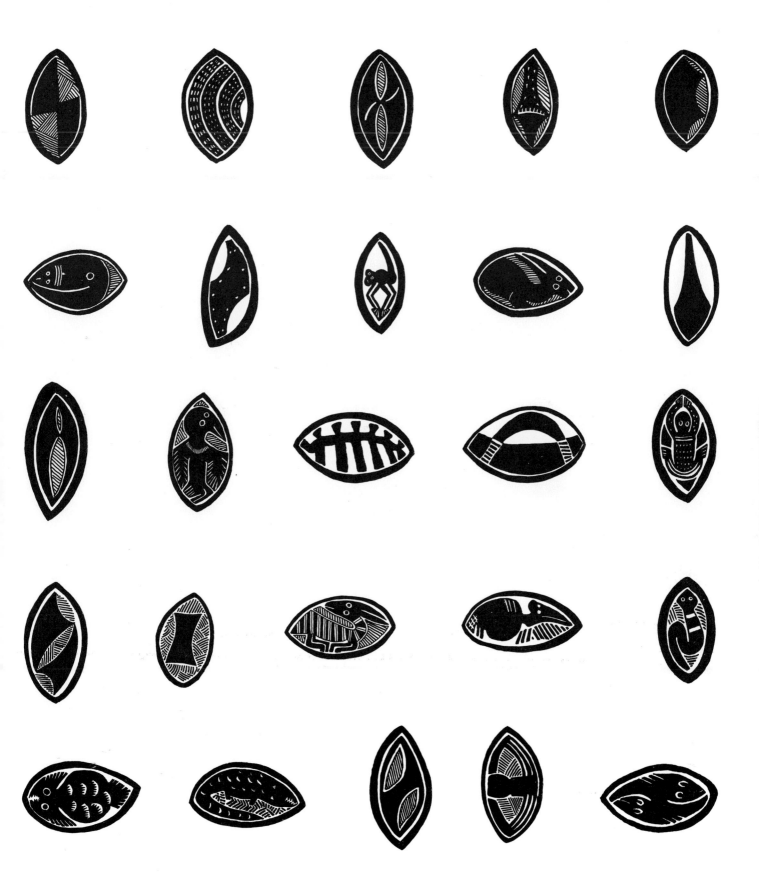

51 Abbia stones, as on the previous page. Among the images carved on the stones are
fish, bats, antelope, shields and monkeys.

52 TOP Two embroidered cotton hats from Sierra Leone. BOTTOM Three caps with woven designs from Senegal or The Gambia.

53 Tanned leather from Mauretania finely decorated with engraved and dyed designs in red and black dye. TOP is a cushion, and BELOW is a leather bag, probably a water bottle.

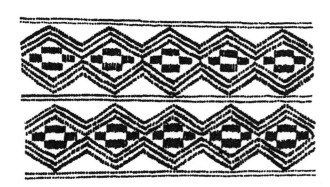

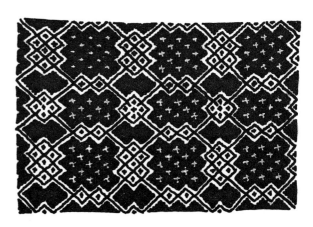

54 Examples of patterns woven by the Manjaka and Papel weavers of Guinea Bissau. The TOP design is an image of Amicar Cabral, who led the nation in its war against the Portuguese. The LOWER designs are largely influenced by Moorish (Moroccan) and Portuguese Renaissance textiles.

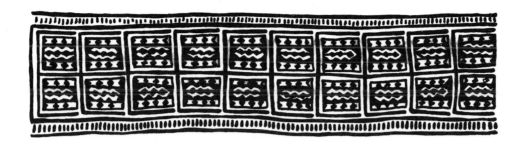

55 The Bambara people of Mali are well known for their 'discharge-dyed' mud cloths. The large number of different patterns used have different names and meanings. The predominant design of the TOP pattern is said to represent the legs and body of the crocodile, with the double zig-zag motif standing for the 'legs of the cricket'.

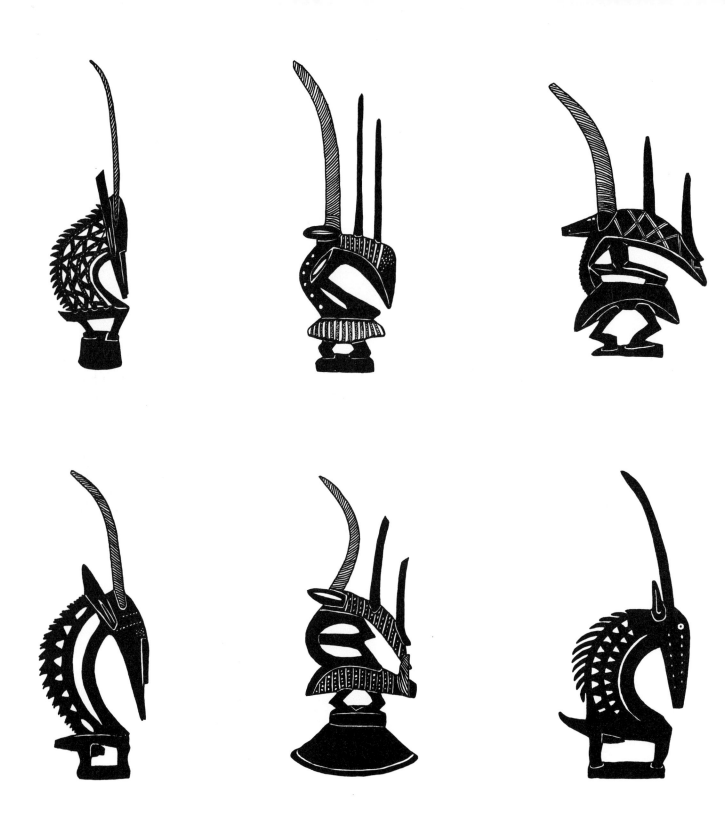

56 These carved wooden antelope headdresses (*Tji wara*) are made by the Bambara (Mali). They represent the mythical antelope who taught man agriculture, and are worn during fertility dances to help the crops grow. TOP LEFT and BOTTOM LEFT and RIGHT show the male antelope, with stylised open-work mane. The others are more abstract designs from the Bougouni District.

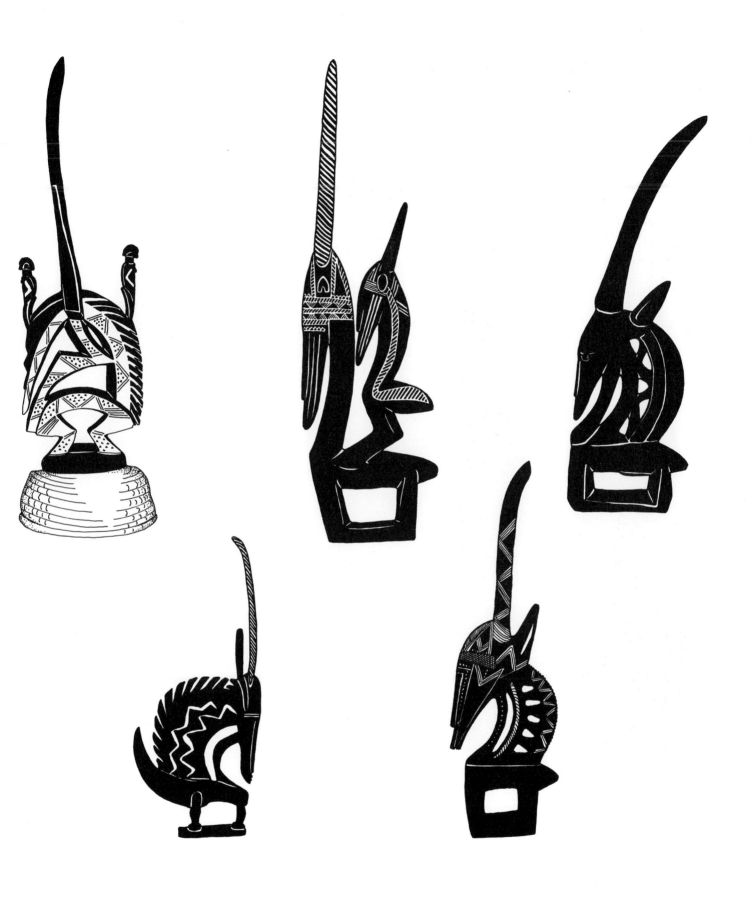

57 Bambara antelope headdresses (*Tji wara*), Mali. The female antelope is depicted with no mane and an offspring on her back (CENTRE). The headdress TOP LEFT has two small human figures on it, and comes from the Bougouni District.

58 Three antelope headdresses (*Tji wara*) drawn to show the detailed patterning which represents hair patterns on the antelope. Bambara, Mali.

59 Motifs on a carved wooden lid from Benin. 16th century.

60 Repoussé decorations on metal, from Benin, 16th century. This methods involves beating the metal with a hammer on the underside so that the pattern is raised on the outer surface. The CENTRE piece is taken from an armlet and shows two Portuguese soldiers.

61 Decorated metal work from Benin (TOP) and Forcados River, southern Nigeria (BELOW). The TOP drawing is the flat end of the King's armrest, the centre of which shows a very formalised head symbolising the Portuguese (see page 67). 16th century. BELOW are two views of a brass bell in the form of an antelope's head. Date unknown, but probably pre-17th century.

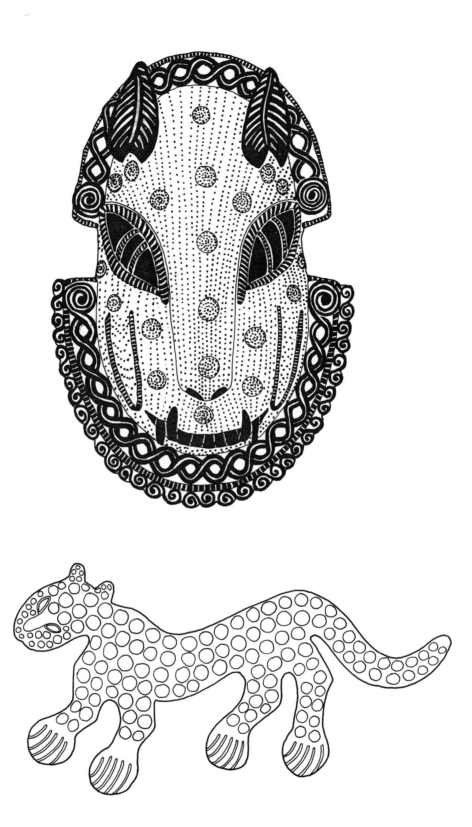

62 TOP A bronze hip mask, worn on the left hip, in the form of a leopard's head. BELOW A leopard made of beaten sheet brass. Benin, 16th century. The leopard was extremely important to the Edo, being King of the Bush, whilst the king (*Oba*) was King of the Home. Only the *Oba* had the right to sacrifice a leopard.

63 TOP and BOTTOM Very fine examples of floral decorations on carved wooden kola nut boxes from Benin, 16th century. The CENTRE piece depicts court figures on a wooden plaque. The LOWER box has four stylised birds with long legs and beaks.

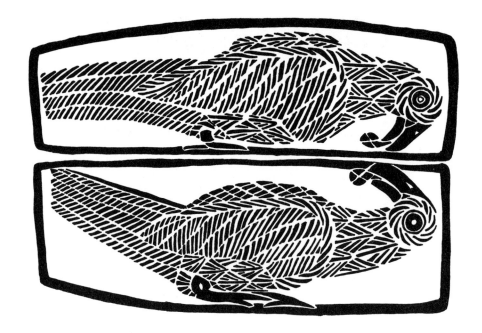

64 Designs taken from carved wooden boxes and a bowl from Benin, 16th century. TOP Two parrots each with a berry in its beak. MIDDLE Leaf patterns on the lid of a bowl. BOTTOM Interlacing pattern along the side of a box, which was a sign of status in Benin.

65 Designs on carved wooden boxes (TOP and MIDDLE two) and a bird from a wooden bowl (BOTTOM). Benin, 16th century. The bird in the TOP design appears to be eating the snake, but probably the snake is issuing from the bird's mouth, a symbol in Edo culture of the spiritually powerful projecting their force into the world.

66 Bronze Benin plaques showing a crocodile eating a fish (TOP) and a fish (BELOW), 16th century. The decoration on the background seems to be the only place where floral forms are found on the plaques. The crocodile is feared for its ferocity and tenaciousness and it represents the extension of the power of the *Oba* (Benin King). Both the *Oba* and the crocodile have the power to take lives.

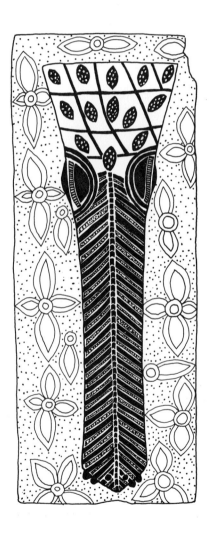

67 Benin bronze plaques showing the floral designs which decorate the background of each one, 16th century. TOP A ceremonial sword, *eben*, carried by court officials. BOTTOM LEFT The head of a crocodile. BOTTOM RIGHT A very naturalistic representation of a Portuguese, with a helmet, long combed hair and a neat beard and moustache.

68 The seat of a Benin bronze stool in the shape of two intwined mudfish (TOP), and a mudfish from a Benin bronze plaque. 16th century. The mudfish is associated with *Olukun*, God of the waters. It represents prosperity, fecundity and peace as opposed to the leopard which represents aggression and conquest (see page 62).

69 Mudfish on Benin bronze plaques, 16th century. The scales and fins of the fish are very finely detailed creating an intricate pattern. Fish are the most common motif found on the plaques.

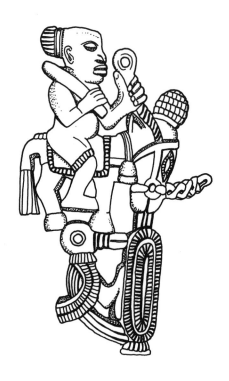

70 Designs taken from carved ivory objects from Benin, 16th century. The CENTRE piece is *Owo*, Yoruba, probably pre-18th century. The BOTTOM RIGHT design is an elephant with its trunk ending in two hands holding leaves, which represents the strength and power of the owner.

71 The Benin ivories are intricately carved with designs of animals. These examples are taken from vessels and drinking cups of the 16th century. In the past all ivory was controlled by the *Oba* (king). It represented strength, longevity and durability and its white colour was a symbol of purity, prosperity and peace.

72 Designs on ivories from Benin, 16th century, and a Yoruba carved ivory box (TOP), pre-18th century. The centre-piece is from a carved elephant tusk which would have been placed at a royal altar.

73 The TOP two drawings come from a carved ivory hunting horn (oliphant) from Sierra Leone, carved by the Sapi. 16th century. BELOW is a figure carved on a 16th-century Benin salt-cellar depicting a richly dressed Portuguese man of *c*.1525–1600, with a long straight beard.

74 Ivory tusks carved with scenes of everyday life and people wearing European dress. Kongo, Zaire, 19th–20th centuries.

23 Tanned leather cushions decorated with printed geometrical pattern motifs and animal forms (TOP and BOTTOM LEFT) Bida, Nupe, Northern Nigeria. BOTTOM RIGHT Cushion embroidered and appliquéd with pieces of leather, probably Hausa, Northern Nigeria.

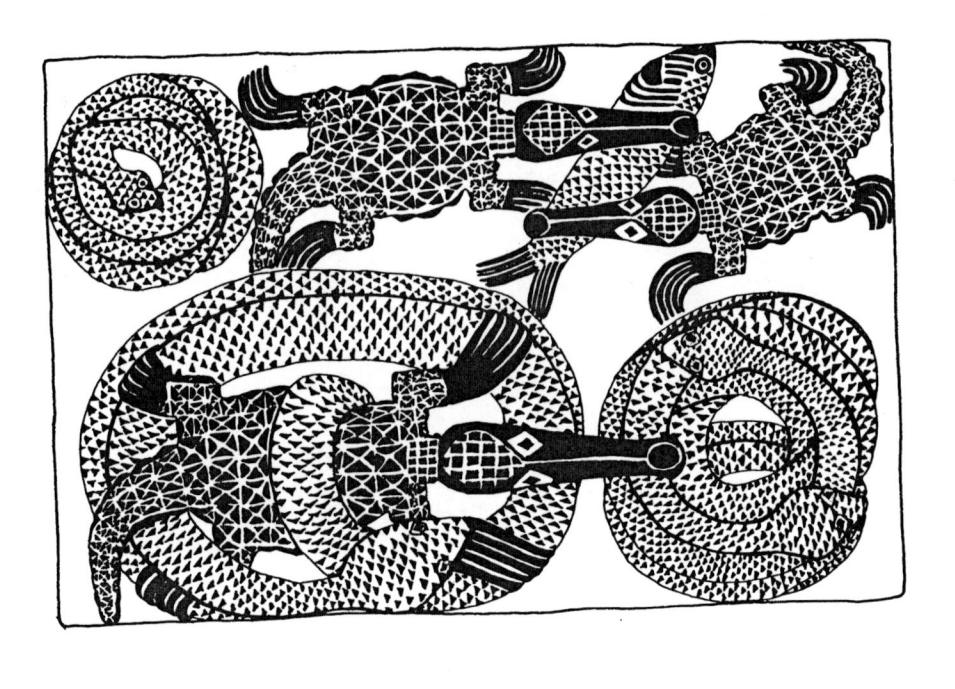

40 These carved wooden boxes from Ghana, on this page and the following few pages, are early examples of 'tourist art'. The boxes show some traditional motifs, and are elaborately decorated with both geometric designs and animal motifs. The LOWER drawing is of the side of a box, the lid of which is shown on page 41.

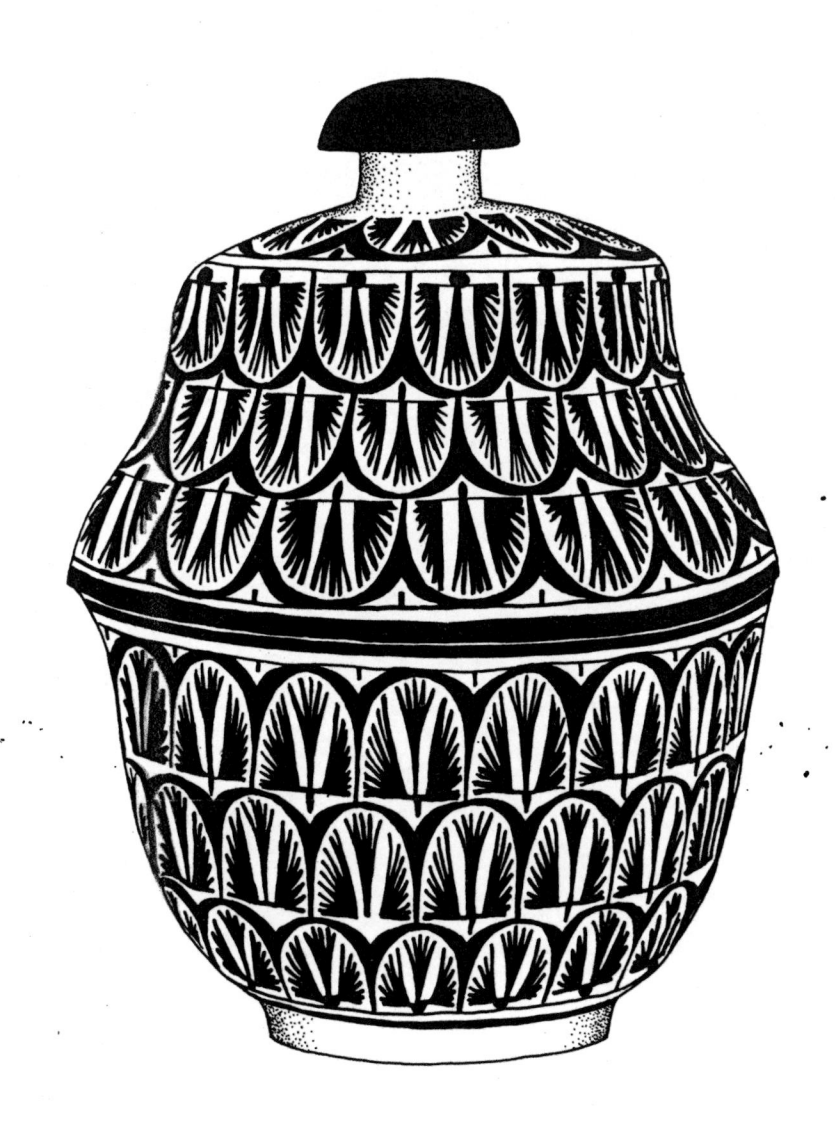

7 Contemporary decorated pottery from Morocco. The TOP jar is in brown and white, and is said to imitate Berber patterns. The BOTTOM vessel with a lid is blue and white.

75 Figures and scenes taken from carved ivory elephant tusks. Zaire, 19th–20th centuries.

76 Figures taken from carved ivory elephant tusks from Boma, Lower Congo, Zaire. These noblemen and women are wearing typical 19th-century European costume copied from newspapers.

77 Figures from carved ivories, 19th century, from Boma, Lower Congo, Zaire. This was one of the regions most exposed to European influence and missionary activity during the 16th century and many of the carved ivories from that period onwards incorporate European figures and Christian symbols.

78 Three decorated calabash and three incised motifs taken from a burnished pottery vessel. All from Lower Congo, Zaire. The patterns on the calabash are made by carving and scraping off the fine layer of the outer skin, leaving white against the natural yellow of the gourd.

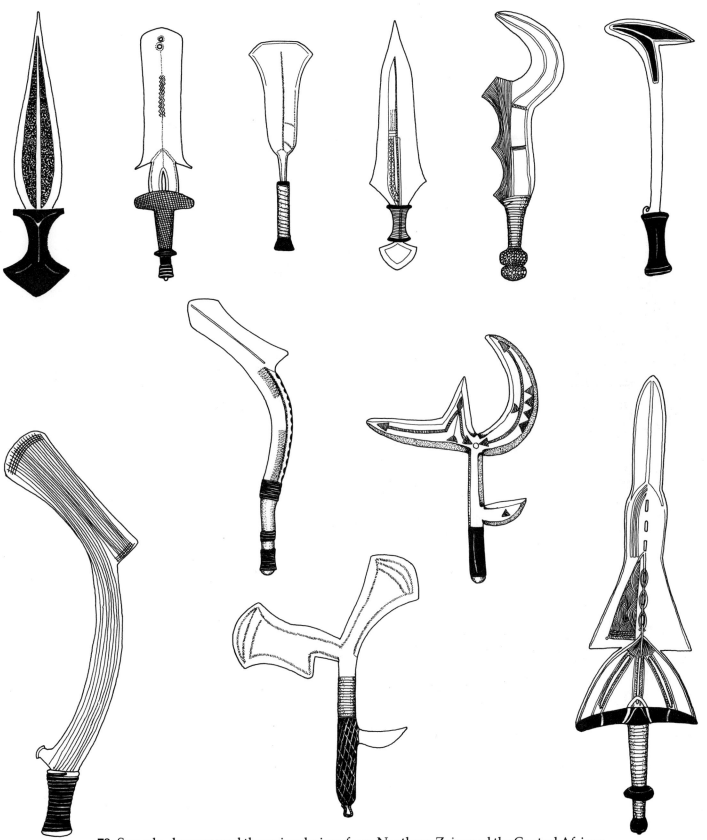

79 Swords, daggers and throwing-knives from Northern Zaire and the Central African Republic. All have decorated metal blades, with wood, leather or copper-bound handles. The extraordinary shapes of some, and the wonderful simplicity of others, again show the relationship between form and pattern, the handle, blade and decoration being designed as one.

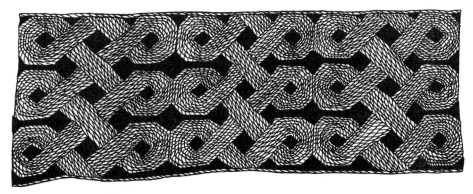

80 The Kuba from Southern Zaire are famous for their 'cut-pile' and embroidered textiles. Their skill is in producing an overall pattern which looks uniform and repetitive, but on closer inspection has subtle variations within it.

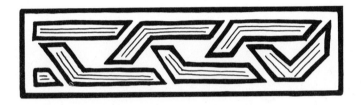

81 Carved wooden boxes made by the Ngongo and Ngeende, Kuba peoples of Southern Zaire. These were carved by men and used by married women to store jewellery and cosmetics.

82 The Kuba from Southern Zaire exhibit an intense love of patterns in every aspect of their material culture, from wood carving, to textiles, to body tattoos. All the different designs have names. These are three carved wooden drinking cups. The one at the TOP is shaped liked two human heads and used for drinking with a guest.

83 Woven mats in two colours probably from Cataracts, Lower Congo. The designs appear in reverse, black on white, on the other sides of the mats. The TOP design is a leopard, the LOWER one shows two people.

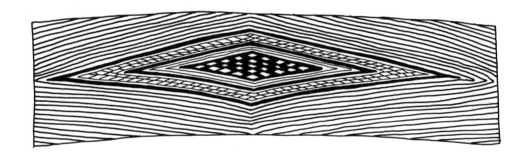

84 Woven raffia border patterns which decorate the edges of Mbuun women's skirts, Southern Zaire.

85 Baskets from Rwanda display striking geometric designs. The weaving is extremely delicate and fine. Some of the patterns have names. The small round flat baskets (TOP) are woven in such a way that the pattern only shows on one side.

86 A coiled basket (TOP) from Kenya, and two wooden stools (BELOW) decorated with
beads. Made by the Luo people, Kenya.

87 Decorated calabash from Kenya. The pattern is made by scorching the surface with a knife or other tool, making it dark brown or black.

88 Dance shields, *ndome*, made by the Kikuyu in Kenya. Boys of the same initiate age-groups and territorial unit had the same patterns on their shields. These patterns would then be used on their war shields when they were initiated.

89 Designs from woven baskets and mats made in Madagascar. These are brightly coloured, using pinks, greens, purples, blues and yellows. They are woven from dyed raffia.

90 Carved wood from Madagascar: two round stools, a decorated box (BOTTOM RIGHT) and a carved window panel (TOP LEFT).

91 Basketware from Zimbabwe: two shallow round baskets (CENTRE), and four table mats. Zimbabwe weavers still use mainly natural-coloured fibres.

92 Carved wooden portable headrests. Shona, Zimbabwe. The headrests form beautiful shapes as well as having detailed patterns carved onto them. They exhibit the maker's eye for achieving the perfect relation between pattern and form.

93 Carved wooden portable headrests. Shona, Zimbabwe.

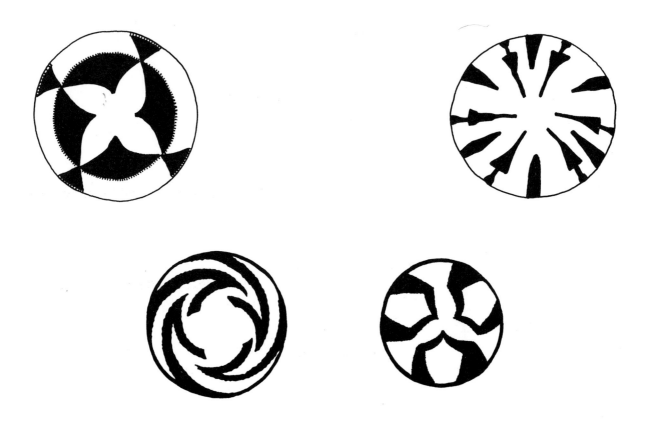

94 Printed textiles from Mochudi, Botswana (TOP) with basket designs, and (BELOW) four woven baskets from the Okovango Delta, with named designs such as (TOP LEFT) 'forehead of the Zebra' and (RIGHT) 'shield'.

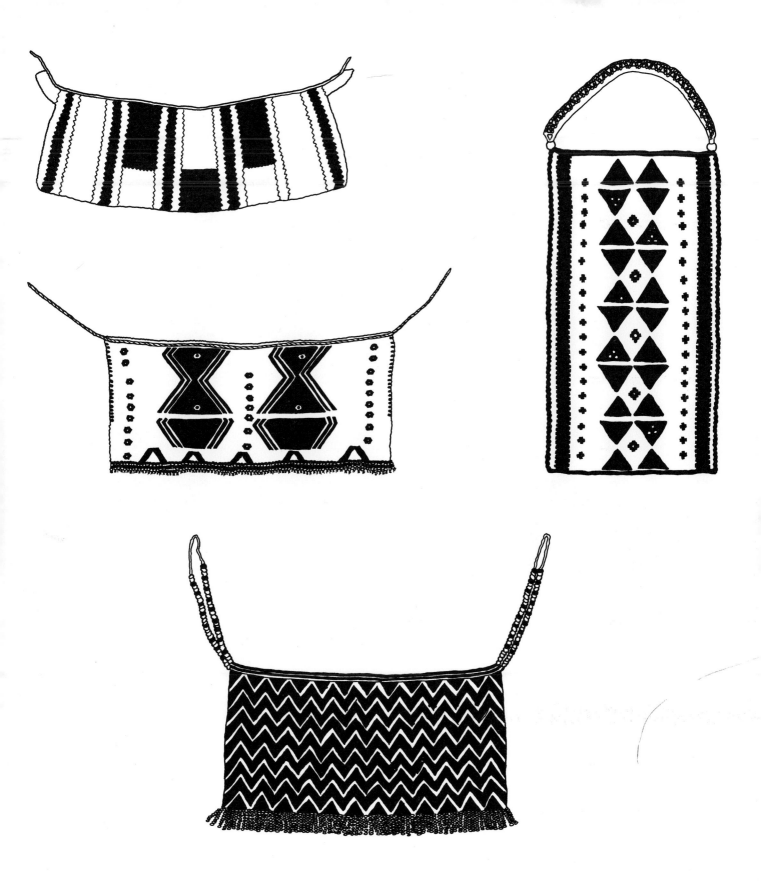

95 Beadwork waistbands from South Africa.

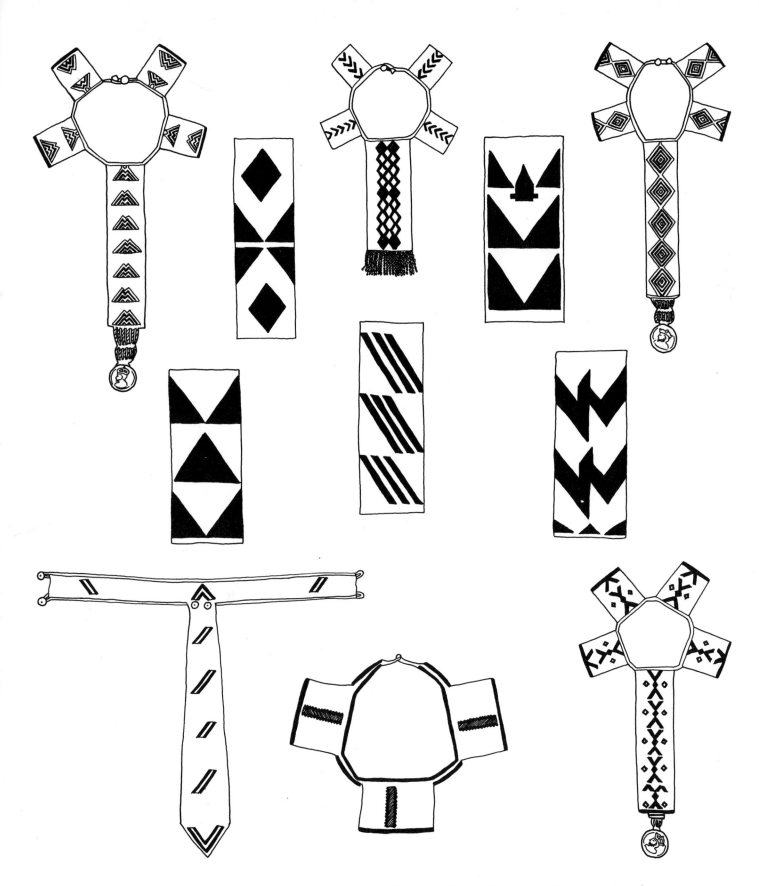

96 Fine beadwork necklaces and anklets made by the Zulu, Zhosa and other peoples of South Africa. Geometrical motifs and interlacing patterns are the most effective bead patterns and many of the designs carry significant messages. LOWER LEFT This necklace is in the shape of a tie.

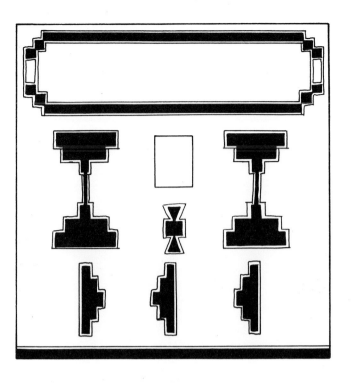

97 Ndbele houses in South Africa are painted by women using symbolic geometric forms, plant and animal shapes and patterns of symmetry. Designs TOP LEFT and BOTTOM RIGHT are of the 'first monochromatic phase', using just grey, black and white. The patterns are often related to patterns of weaving, and the paintings embellish the structure of the house.

98 Designs from murals on houses, South Africa. The top two Sotho designs are applied to walls using a scraper (a knife or a fork) giving the added effect of texture as well as colour to the mural. The scraping gives the effect of ploughed fields. The simple four-petalled pattern (BOTTOM LEFT) forms the basis of many Sotho designs. These patterns would be repeated so that a whole wall is covered.

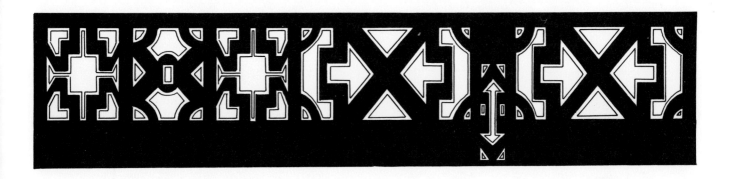

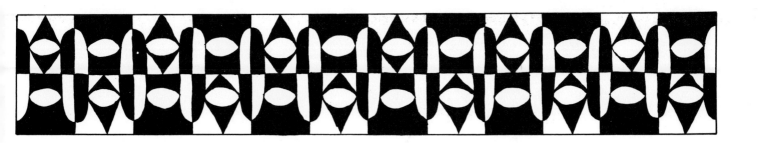

99 Mural designs from South Africa. TOP A border pattern in the Sotho-Ndbele style which runs along the top of a wall. MIDDLE A First-Phase Ndbele mural, decorating the entire length of the side of a house, with black-and-white geometric designs. BOTTOM A wall painted by Matuel Dani from the Orange Free State.

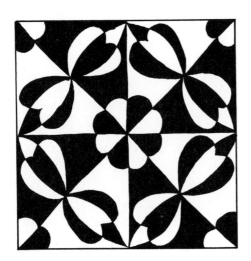 

100 The TOP design was found on the same wall as the design on page 99 (BOTTOM), but has been re-painted. MIDDLE LEFT shows a typical Sotho design and MIDDLE RIGHT is from Southern Sotho, a flower design covering the whole side of one wall. The fish is from northern Lesotho where the Ndbele and Sotho designs merge, the suburban influence affecting the traditional style.